# THE LIQUIDATION OF THE
# BRITISH EMPIRE

# The Liquidation of the British Empire

*The Reid Lectures
of Acadia University 1959*

by

## C. E. CARRINGTON

M.A. (Oxon. et Cantab.)

*Professor of British Commonwealth Relations
Royal Institute of International Affairs*

with a Foreword by

## WATSON KIRKCONNELL

Ph.D. LL.D. D.P.Ec. D.Litt. Litt.D. L.H.D.

*President of Acadia University Nova Scotia*

## GEORGE G. HARRAP & CO. LTD

LONDON   TORONTO   WELLINGTON   SYDNEY

*First published in Great Britain* 1961
*by* GEORGE G. HARRAP & CO. LTD
182 High Holborn, London, W.C.1

© *C. E. Carrington* 1961

*Composed in Bell type and printed by*
*Western Printing Services Ltd, Bristol*
*Made in Great Britain*

# Foreword

THE Reid Lectures were established in 1958 by Harvey T. Reid, B.A. (Acadia and Oxon.), D.C.L. (Acadia), of Saint Paul, Minnesota. Their purpose is to bring to Acadia University, at least every second year, some eminent scholar or man of affairs who will give a brief series of lectures on some important phase of history or political science. Their founder expressed a basic preference for some theme related to the British Commonwealth of Nations, but did not rigidly so restrict the lecturer.

Dr Reid was born in Hartland, New Brunswick, in 1891 and entered Acadia University in 1908. On graduating in 1912 he was chosen as Rhodes Scholar for Nova Scotia and took an Oxford degree two years later. In the First World War he served as a captain in the Royal Field Artillery and was wounded in action. In due time he became a member of the Minnesota State Bar Association and the American Bar Association. He has been president of the West Law Publishing Company since 1948 and of the American Law Book Publishing Company since 1952.

An invitation to deliver the first Reid Lectures was given early in 1958 to His Excellency Norman A. Robertson, Canadian Ambassador to the U.S.A. and formerly High Commissioner to the United Kingdom. His lectures were entitled "Some Thoughts on the Commonwealth."

Charles Edmund Carrington, M.A. (Oxon. et Cantab.), who delivered the second series of lectures in October 1959, is Professor of British Commonwealth Relations in the Royal Institute of International Affairs, Chatham House, London.  Receiving his early education in New Zealand, he matriculated at Oxford shortly before the outbreak of the First World War, in which he served in France and Italy, won the Military Cross, and rose to the rank of captain.  He was an assistant master at Haileybury College for several years, then joined the Cambridge University Press in 1929 and in time became its educational manager.  In the Second World War he again saw service and was a lieutenant-colonel on the General Staff, 1941–45. A long devotion to historical research and publication gave rise to such volumes as *A History of England* (with Hampden Jackson, 1932), *An Exposition of Empire* (1947), *The British Overseas* (1950), and *Godley of Canterbury* (1951).

His Reid Lectures, *The Liquidation of the British Empire*, give a spirited reply to certain views of British policy that are often current in the United States.  He expresses a reasoned confidence in the future of Central Africa.

WATSON KIRKCONNELL

PRESIDENT'S OFFICE
  ACADIA UNIVERSITY
    WOLFVILLE
      NOVA SCOTIA

*June* 1960

## Preface

THIS little book is based upon three lectures delivered in October 1959 at Acadia University. I have made no substantial alterations, but have rearranged the material for publication. I take this opportunity of thanking the President and the Staff of Acadia University for their hospitality.

C. E. CARRINGTON

CHATHAM HOUSE
  LONDON

*January* 1961

# Contents

# I

## Empire to Commonwealth

AT the climax of the Second World War, when the
shadow of defeat for the Grand Alliance had receded and the prospect of victory was coming up
like dawn over a distant horizon, Winston Churchill made
one of his celebrated pronouncements at a ceremony in
London. For generations it has been customary for the
Prime Minister of Great Britain to use his annual appear-
ance at the Lord Mayor's Banquet as the occasion for a
policy statement, and Churchill, with his deep historical
sense, was no doubt thinking of heroic words delivered by
Pitt on earlier Lord Mayor's Days when he said, "I have
not become the King's First Minister in order to preside
over the liquidation of the British Empire."[1]

These brave words were variously received at home
and abroad. In Britain they came, like many of Churchill's
words, as a heartener. The British remembered that in the
dark days of 1940 and 1941 they had not stood alone in the
defence of liberty; they had been supported by the free and
generous alliance of a world-wide Commonwealth and
Empire, which in 1943 was for the most part still intact.
It was weakened, impoverished, deprived of some limbs,
but still stable and secure, and it was now looking forward

to recovery. What had been lost while so much had been saved? There was the secession of Ireland to be shown on the debit side of the account. It was felt in London to be deplorable that Ireland should dissociate herself, by withdrawing into neutralism, on so straightforward an issue as that between liberty and aggressive fascism; yet no irrevocable harm had been done. Bitterness between England and Ireland had lessened, and in 1943 the last constitutional links had not been snapped. The ancient feud might still be ended with time and patience.

But, at the other end of the world, a blow had been struck at British power from which Western imperialism in Asia could not recover. The capture of Singapore by the Japanese in February 1942 was a far greater disaster to the Commonwealth and Empire as a whole and, accordingly, to Britain as an imperial power than the evacuation of Dunkirk. Something had been finally 'liquidated' at Singapore, and not all the King's horses nor all the King's men could restore it.

When Churchill spoke these words all the dependent territories of Britain, France, the Netherlands, and the United States in South-east Asia were under Japanese military control. The campaigns to recover these territories were afoot, and there was already a remarkable difference of opinion among the Allies as to the future status of such areas after they were liberated. Few people in Britain were aware, however, of the upsurge of anti-colonial opinion in the United States. To the British, as to the French and Dutch, the expulsion of the Japanese invaders would lead to no other result than the restoration of legitimate governments which had existed before the war. They were surprised and pained to learn, indirectly and by hints and allusions, that their American allies took a very different view. Imperialism was a subject upon which American opinion was ill-informed, even in the highest circles. The strangest notions were current of the nature and tendency of British colonial rule, and Franklin Roosevelt in particular seemed to have heard of nothing that had happened in the British territories in Asia in the previous fifty years. It was his suggestion[2] that the loyal colony of Hongkong, when liberated, should be handed over to the corrupt and unrepresentative administration of Chiang-Kai-shek, apparently in accordance with some undefined principle of natural justice, that provoked Winston Churchill's statement. In Churchill's view the British colonial system was to be restored when victory had been won, in order that it might proceed smoothly along the well-worn path from Empire to Commonwealth. Though this proved not so easy, the free world and the people of Hongkong may at least be thankful that Churchill's rejection of Roosevelt's monstrous suggestion saved Hongkong from the fate of Shanghai; it has given Hongkong fourteen years of liberty and prosperity.

Proud though we may be of having liberated Hongkong and preserved it in liberty, we are obliged to admit that it is an exceptional instance. Generally speaking, the European empires in Asia either did not survive the war or were liquidated during the twelve years that followed it; that is if I may give my own meaning to the vogue-word 'liquidate.' Almost everywhere there has been a transfer of power, except in some remote and backward islands where the inhabitants as yet have made insufficient technical progress to justify political progress. I do not propose to linger on the creation of new independent states in Burma,

Ceylon, the Indian subcontinent, or Malaya, beyond making two observations, the first on their status, the second on the constitutional process by which they achieved self-government. Each of these states has a long history; in each we may observe the reappearance of a nationality long submerged. These countries, which succumbed a century or two centuries ago to the superior techniques of European invaders, profited by their experience and acquired a sufficient mastery of those techniques to compete with their conquerors.

The Republic of India came into existence with an administration that had long commanded the admiration of the world, and that was substantially Indianized except in the higher political appointments. The system of communications by road, rail, and telegraph was unrivalled in Asia and was superior to that of some European countries. Twenty great universities, the oldest of them approaching their centennial year, were sending out more than 40,000 graduates per annum[3] to swell the large class of highly educated Indians—a small proportion of the whole people, but nevertheless a very large body of educated persons. The external debts of India had been repatriated during the wartime years, which had brought, as well as hideous misfortunes, a temporary flow of prosperity to the growers of primary products. And India, for all its backwardness and poverty, was well on the road towards industrialism, with steel-works and heavy engineering plants owned and operated by Indians. It had, in short, reached what Professor W. Rostow describes as the "taking-off point." With a mature economy India was ripe—indeed, over-ripe—for a mature political system. The British cannot be criticized for withholding political advantages from India in the last days of the British-Indian Empire. On the contrary, many good judges would say that they moved too fast. It was at an earlier stage that more enterprising steps towards self-government might have been taken. From 1906 until 1922 Great Britain was ruled by Liberal statesmen who proposed, in other fields, remarkably enlightened and farsighted programmes. Their Indian policy, in retrospect, seems weak and timid. But a historian should never allow himself to reproach his forerunners for failing to predict the future, and before 1914 no one had the least conception of the fundamental changes that would transform international affairs as a consequence of the events of that disastrous year.

No other territory in southern Asia was, or is, as far advanced in technological development as the Republic of India, but analogous progress had been made in several other countries, notably Burma and Ceylon, each of them in the 1930s a prosperous and, by Asian standards, well-educated state, and each endowed with a constitution embodying the principle of representative government. Both were still far from independence, but both had taken the first steps on the path that had already brought the old Dominions to full national status.

This is the first comment that I propose to make about the liquidation of the British Empire in Asia. The social, economic, and administrative infra-structure of a nation-state already existed in these countries. The sense of nationality was based upon ancient and valid tradition. History and culture had already in great part been reviewed and interpreted in the light of Western education; the mechanism of a modern technological society had been brought into existence; indigenous experts in most fields of activity had been trained (not enough of them, of course, but there never are enough); and all was ready for the transfer of power when the fever of resurgent nationalism demanded it.

The degree of preparedness and the resources available, both in men and materials, varied from territory to territory. Accordingly, the smoothness with which the transfer of power was accomplished also varied. It is no part of my purpose to discuss the politics of independent Asia, not even such portentous events as the partition of the Indian subcontinent. I observe that, while the political systems devised by the British have in some cases failed to survive the withdrawal of British power, there is at present no instance in which the social infra-structure, which I have tried to describe in a few words, has collapsed. What was transferred was a going concern, and in every one of these countries it still goes.

My second comment is that every transfer of power by the British in Asia was effected by a strictly legal process. The appalling bloodshed that accompanied the partition of the Indian subcontinent and the long refusal of the Congress Party to co-operate in the intermediate stages of self-government have had the effect of presenting the recent history of India and Pakistan as a revolution; that is to say, a violent breach with the past leading to the creation of a wholly new system based upon a different sanction. It is likely that the historical myth-makers in Asia will rewrite the story of their countries in these terms, and they may even be justified in doing so. But a constitutional lawyer relating the histories of Burma, Ceylon, and Malaya must describe these processes in terms of the gradual decentralization of power by authority of the

Parliament of the United Kingdom according to precedents made in the earlier cases of Canada, Australia, New Zealand, and South Africa.

Now a word must be said about the sanctions of political authority, in exposition of a thesis which might be more readily accepted by Canadians than by Englishmen. No one, not even the Americans, can now regard Canada as a dependency of Great Britain, and yet the Canadian Constitution is still, in legal form, embodied in a British Act of Parliament. So far as it has been invited to do so, the Parliament of the United Kingdom has divested itself of authority to legislate for Canada,[4] and no circumstances can be foreseen in which the British would search for residual fragments of true legislative power, unless the Canadian Government should invite them to co-operate in finding a way of escape from some legal entanglement. The transfer of power was long since complete, but a federal state must have a written constitution and must deposit the title-deeds in some safe place. Various devices have been used to ensure that the fundamentals of a federal constitution shall not be overthrown by some party pursuing sectional interests while enjoying temporary power. In Canada the stability of the Constitution has been ensured by lodging it in a safe-deposit outside the jurisdiction, or rather, to speak more precisely, by allowing it to remain in the safe-deposit where it was lodged by the former Imperial power almost a century ago. The sanction of the Canadian Constitution, therefore, lies in positive law as interpreted by the Canadian courts, with no provision for any further appeal. It is rooted in the past, and Canada has shown no disposition hitherto to cut the tap-root.

B

In the eyes of a lawyer this is true of every state within the British Commonwealth of Nations. It is true of India and Pakistan, which have adopted republican instead of monarchical forms of executive power, and of South Africa and Rhodesia, where the civil law derives from the Roman-Dutch code. The continuity of the legal system is taken for granted by the courts and is valued by the legal profession. Even the Indian Constitution, that elaborate monument of legal and political learning, reveals in clause after clause its debt to earlier British legislation and notably to the Government of India Act of 1935.[5] Indian constitutional history, if it could be divorced from political history, would be seen as a continuous process in which each step followed logically from the last, some steps, of course, being giant strides.

If I may be thought to be stretching a point in the case of India I need make no concession to my critics in the cases of Ceylon and Malaya. In neither of these countries was there a national revolt, and power was transferred in both instances by friendly agreement with administrations that had already enjoyed some measure of power.

The constitutional processes by which Malayan independence was achieved in 1957 are of peculiar interest. Like the Constitution of Canada, the Malayan Constitution is embodied in a document issued through normal channels by authority of the Crown.[6] It restored full independence to certain Malayan states which had voluntarily accepted British protection at various dates during the last century, and on its own authority it combined them into a federation, to which two small colonies with constitutions of a different type also adhered. It also created a wholly new type of federal government. The system required a series of compromises and legal fictions of the kind which political scientists rigorously trained in the logical clarity of the Roman Law find incomprehensible, and which lawyers trained in the flexible and accommodating English common law interpret without much difficulty in the courts. It is a special instance of the type of constitution which has served as a starting-point for so many colonial countries on their way to independence.

Among its numerous complications the Constitution of Malaya presents three features which may be worth our attention. First, it created a new monarchy within the Commonwealth and expressly stated that the allegiance of Malayan citizens would in future be due to the Yang di-Pertuan Agong, not to the Queen of Great Britain. At the same time the appeal to the Privy Council, which had been abolished in most of the older Commonwealth countries, was retained in Malaya, so that to that extent the residual authority of the British Crown survived. Secondly, the adherence of the former Straits Settlements—Penang and Malacca—to the Malayan Federation required that the Queen should absolve the inhabitants of these countries from the allegiance they had formerly borne her as British subjects. Thirdly, this complex and unusual instrument was neither drawn up, like the Canadian Constitution, by a conference of local experts, nor was it imposed, like the Constitution of New Zealand, by experts from the Colonial Office. It was prepared by a committee of experts from all parts of the Commonwealth. It is indeed an interesting and original document on which further remarks may be made. Its form is wholly in the tradition of the English common law; its method of enactment and enforcement is in accordance with the usual British procedure; and, whatever may be its future, it has served its purpose by launching Malaya into independence with no disruption of the legal or social fabric.

I must not press my case too hard. Although the political history of Australia has been placid, quite remarkably free of the violent and bloody upheavals that make up so much of the so-called drama of history in less fortunate lands, there was an unusual precedent in the story of Australian confederation. Bryce's great work on the United States[7] had been recently published when the Australian founding fathers set to work in the 1890s. It made a great impression on contemporary thought, with the consequence that certain fundamental features of American political philosophy found their way into the Australian Constitution, whereas they had been wholly absent from the Constitution of Canada.

The method of establishing the Commonwealth of Australia rather resembled the method by which a territory such as Alaska comes to full membership in the United States. The constitutional instrument was home-made, and before being submitted to the British Parliament it was referred back to a plebiscite in each of the Australain states. It thus obtained a new sanction. Its legal force was derived, like that of the Constitution of Canada, from a British Act of Parliament;[8] its moral force came directly from the will of the Australian people, a large majority of whom had voted in its favour. Accordingly, the preamble included a solemn reference to the source of authority, not omitting an appeal for the blessing of Almighty God upon the new nation then brought into existence. Analogous appeals to first principles are to be found in the resolutions by which the constituent assemblies in India and Pakistan initiated their work.[9]

It may well be thought that the direct sanction of the democratic principle is in accord with the spirit of the twentieth century. Be this so or not, the constitutional lawyer will dryly assert that it makes not the slightest difference to the processes of jurisdiction. No one supposes that Canada, where the Constitution is based upon the British North America Act, is any less free than Australia, where the Constitution was adopted by a referendum. The continuity of constitutional development and of legal procedure is common to both. Neither country was 'liberated,' and if we are to speak of the liquidation of the British Empire we must add that the same ingredients, when the Empire was dissolved, were allowed to crystallize again as the British Commonwealth. At no point in the legal process was there a radical revolutionary change. This is true of Ceylon and Malaya, and, within the limits of my argument, it is even to some extent true of India. But all these states were formed communities: in all, the infrastructure of society was secure, the nation was conscious of its self-sufficiency, and no enlightened person doubted that the transfer of power was inevitable. The questions to be answered were *how*, *when*, and *to whom?*

To judge from the diatribes against colonialism that are to be heard so frequently in the Trusteeship Committee at the United Nations it might be supposed that these questions were easy to answer. Power should be transferred here and now to nations rightly struggling to be free. Is not the sacred principle of self-determination written into the Charter?

Self-determination is a word with an amusing history. As a term in metaphysics relating to the doctrine of free will it was used by several philosophers of the eighteenth century. About fifty years ago it was adopted by Lenin and, more particularly, by Trotsky[10] as part of the jargon of revolutionary socialism, and as such it appears in the great *Oxford English Dictionary*, where it is given the reference: "*Self-determination*—The Bolshevist theory." The term came to the notice of President Woodrow Wilson and was used by him in several political speeches in 1917 when alluding to the liberation of Poland and Czechoslovakia as a war aim of the Allies. Contrary to popular belief, the word does not occur in his manifesto to the world which is remembered as the Fourteen Points. None of his senior advisers liked the President's new slogan very much. The Secretary of State's comment was: "What a calamity the phrase was ever uttered! What misery it will cause!" Later the President himself repented of it.[11]

In spite of an effort by the President's adviser Colonel House to insert it into the first draft of the Charter for the League of Nations it was excluded, and the draft that was finally accepted made a distinction between the status of the oppressed nations of Europe and that of the backward territories in Africa and elsewhere which were not yet ripe for self-government. For the colonies of the defeated German Empire the new mandatory principle (to which we now give the name trusteeship) was devised, and the word self-determination fell into disfavour. When the Royal Institute of International Affairs was founded at Chatham House the leading article in the first number of its quarterly journal was a scholarly refutation by the great liberal, Gilbert Murray, of the principle of self-determination; the problem of applying it, he said, was "theoretically and practically insoluble."[12] What, precisely, did the word mean? It could imply nothing but the supposed right of any compact and dissident minority group to break away from the larger community and form an independent state. If Ireland has a right of self-determination against England, so has Ulster a right against Ireland, and the county of Fermanagh against Ulster. Why stop here? Does self-determination mean the right of every citizen to defy a law he disapproves of? We need not reduce the disputation *ad absurdum*. Did not the greatest statesman of the nineteenth century, Abraham Lincoln, burst this bubble when he declared that, with or without slavery, he would preserve the Union?

Somehow or other the refuted doctrine crept back into popularity in 1945, and the statesmen at San Francisco, so much less wise than their forerunners at Versailles, admitted this dangerous term to the Charter of the United Nations, with precisely the consequence that had been earlier foreseen. The world has been Balkanized, fragmented into a great and ever-growing number of states, many of them so small and weak that using their nuisance-value in the Assembly is their main contribution to world affairs.

We may see in the world to-day two contradictory processes at work. On the one hand, nationalism run rabid, the ignoble demands of small linguistic groups to cut themselves off from the main stream of progress under the pitiful slogan of Sinn Fein—"Ourselves alone." On the other hand, the multiplication of international and cosmopolitan links between the advanced countries where it is recognized that nationalism is an atavistic force, a relic of past and worse days, a doctrine that the world has outgrown and should leave behind.

To say so when addressing an academic audience may be useful for touching off a discussion on first principles in politics. There are audiences in Asia and Africa where the crude statement just made would provoke a riot. It is useless, as the King says in *Love's Labour's Lost*, to march against "the huge army of the world's desires." The emotional force of anti-colonialism has risen to so high a pitch throughout the world, among simple and backward tribes as well as among nations that, in the course of history, have temporarily lost their former autonomy, that demands for self-government can no longer be denied. No one any longer willingly submits to government by a foreign power, however beneficent and well-intentioned it may be, except on the understanding that the administration is a temporary stopgap while an autonomous government is being organized. Thus we see, on the one hand, that Soviet Russia required for the control of an oppressed nation, Hungary, an army of occupation greater than the whole strength of the British Army; while, on the other hand, British colonial statesmen in all parts of the world—in the West Indies, in Nigeria, in the Rhodesias, in Borneo—are feverishly working to create the machinery for administering new national groups. In the case of Hungary, the solution would be simple. Here the principle of self-determination would apply since no one doubts that Hungary, by its linguistic and cultural traditions, by its long autonomous history, by its formed administration and its mature economy, presents all the features of a nation-state. All that is needed is to liberate Hungary so that it may resume its former co-operation with its neighbours. Without Hungary, Europe is incomplete; with Hungary restored, the international situation would be more stable. Here self-determination and progress would march together.

But in Rhodesia, Nigeria, and the West Indies the situation is wholly different. Plans are now well forward in each of these regions for the grouping together of small societies belonging to different tribes and races or separated on distant islands into larger, viable communities which may eventually coalesce and form nations. This is a question not of breaking down old empires but of building new and larger states. The problem is not to set them free from foreign rule but to induce them to combine for common ends under indigenous rulers. A popular vote may suffice to carry a well-organized racial or tribal group into association with a nation-state, but if the nation-state has never existed and does not yet exist the vote for self-determination is worthless, indeed meaningless. A new nation cannot be voted into existence without organs or members or even a tongue.

If, then, I reject self-determination as an ill-conceived slogan foisted upon the Commonwealth at a late stage in its growth, can I find historical warrant for the lawyers' concept of continuous constitutional progress? It would be absurd to claim that it tells the whole story, but it tells a part of it and a part that should not be overlooked. The world is well acquainted now with the theory of the Statute of Westminster Commonwealth, concerning the group of Dominions whose status was recognized during the First World War and defined in the Balfour Declaration of 1926.[13] To sustain my thesis I must answer two questions: how far back can we trace the application of the theory of Dominion status in the colonies by settlement? And what evidence is there of an intention to apply the principle of Dominion status to the colonies by conquest and cession, particularly to the colonies inhabited by Asians and Africans? If there has been no deliberate plan to develop self-governing constitutions and to extend them to a widening circle of territories, the liquidation of the British Empire must be regarded as a destructive revolution.

My first question can be answered by examining the history of Canada. When the House of Commons was debating the Constitutional Act of 1791,[14] the first statutory grant of self-government in British colonial history, speaker after speaker declared—not without naïve complacency—that the purpose of the Bill was to give the Canadians the greatest blessing in the world, a constitution like that of Britain's. Henry Dundas, one of the Secretaries of State, made the significant observation that "they could not pretend to give Canada the same constitution that they themselves lived under; all they could do was to lay the foundation for the same constitution, when increased population and time should have made the Canadians ripe to receive it."[15] The Canadian Constitution, like the British Constitution, had a principle of growth in it; in time it would weld the Canadians into a nation. As readers of Canadian history know, the Constitution of 1791 was no great success, but it was a step in the right direction, and during the next 170 years parliamentary draughtsmen had plenty of practice in improving upon it. Lord Durham hit upon the most useful device when he recommended what is called responsible government. The men of 1864 and 1865 completed the pattern when they solved the racial problem in Canada by federation. In 1867, after a long period of trial and error, the objective, so clearly defined in 1791, was reached at last.

The same objective, achieved by a progress from representative government to responsible government, federation, and independent status within the Commonwealth, lay before the peoples of Nigeria in 1960 and lies before the West Indies in 1961. The historical analogy is perfect.

To answer my second question I must look back to see what was happening in the other dependencies of the Crown during the years when the old Dominions matured to potential, if not actual, independence. Read back among books and articles published in the 1920s and 1930s and you will find the focus of attention upon a limited number of subjects. While there was much academic discussion on the precise status of the Dominions, it would be idle to pretend that this was a matter on which political feeling ran high except in South Africa and Ireland. When the House of Commons discussed Imperial problems at Westminster, the prominent topic was the future of India. On this subject there was much expert opinion to be tapped, sharp division between political parties, and strong emotional reactions throughout the instructed part of the electorate. I do not propose to recall now the various acts and scenes of the Indian drama between 1919 and 1947 when the decision for immediate independence was made, but merely to suggest that the Government of India Act of 1935 placed in the hands of the peoples of India the power to work their own way to independence by the path Canada had taken after the Constitutional Act of 1791. The virtue of the Act of 1935 lay not so much in what it gave, as in the use to which it could be put. That path was rejected by the Indian Congress Party, and, eventually also by the Moslem League, on the grounds that the Act came too late and gave too little. The time was ripe in the view of the Indian statesmen who led the majority parties for an immediate transfer of power into their hands. An imposed constitution at this late date in Indian history, however enlightened in principle, however expertly adapted, would no longer serve. The Indian nation was mature and must decide its own fate. It did so, at the cost of partition, and the massacre of scores of thousands of people.

Meanwhile, a process of gradual constitutional advancement moved with remarkable smoothness in Ceylon, and, a few years later, was repeated in Malaya. From these events and from the history of India, constitutional lawyers and political leaders learned different lessons.

The lawyers observed that the infra-structure persisted, both in India and Pakistan; that the type of constitution which they had designed for undivided India was adopted with suitable modification by both countries after partition; and that all had gone more nearly according to plan in the simpler circumstances of Ceylon and Malaya.

The leaders of popular politics learned different lessons. They observed that Mahatma Gandhi and Mr Nehru had prevailed and triumphed by non-co-operation and by courting martyrdom; that the emotions engendered by these heroes in their struggle for a defiant liberty had endowed them with power securely based upon the popular will; and that national enthusiasm was born from sufferings endured in a struggle for liberation. A dangerous course to imitate!

During the same years the region known in Britain as the Middle East passed through a series of transformations, the history of which has not yet been written. At the end of the First World War the victorious British had been left in military occupation of almost the whole world of Islam, from Sarawak to Nigeria, their only rivals in power being the French. They quickly disembarrassed themselves of a large part of this unprofitable commitment, but emerged from the peace settlement with a protectorate over Egypt, and with mandates for Iraq, Jordan, and Palestine under the Charter of the League of Nations. British relations with these four countries have bedevilled international politics for forty years. Let us for a moment forget the sad story of the Palestine mandate, that perpetual warning against philanthropy at other people's expense, and let us defer the history of Egyptian independence for consideration later. The forgotten achievements of those forty years are that Britain liberated Iraq and Jordan from their Turkish oppressors, founded and established their national institutions, nourished these infant nations in strict accordance with the terms of the mandate, and launched them into independence without violent pressure either from internal or external forces. Both countries owe their existence and such prosperity as they possess to Britain, and it seemed not unreasonable to expect that they should remain, when independent, in a treaty relationship with Britain similar to that between the United States and the Philippine Republic. But some hideous fate seemed to blast the efforts and to mock the good intentions of the British in the Middle East. All went awry, not only in Palestine where gross errors had been made in the original planning, not only in Egypt where there was a legacy of historical hatreds, but in Iraq and Jordan where there were no such handicaps. There is no gratitude in politics. The notion, ascribed to T. E. Lawrence, that there might be in the Middle East a group of self-governing brown Dominions associated as freely with the British Empire as the white Dominions proved to be mere moonshine.[16]

I now turn to the colonial Empire properly speaking. Sir Winston Churchill, in the last days of the War, used to refer with deliberation to the Commonwealth and Empire. If Canada and Australia could no longer be correctly described as dependencies of an Empire, obviously there were many other territories that still could be so described. The mere effect of drawing the distinction made it unpalatable to those territories. What neither Churchill nor, so far as I know, anyone else foresaw in 1943 was the instant universal demand from every colony, however weak and backward, to be acknowledged as being of the same status as the great self-reliant, self-supporting, and self-governing Dominions.

Before the War left-wing parties in several countries had denounced the imperialist powers for what was called the exploitation of subject races, but the remedy the radicals proposed for the wrongs of Africa, in particular, was to bring the colonies under international control. There had also been sporadic agitations for a Pan-African movement, but its supporters were to be found mostly in America or Europe. For the most part Africa, or at least tropical Africa between the Limpopo river and the Sahara Desert, was unawakened and unconscious of the democratic upsurge in Asia.

In 1939 the white Dominions had attained full independence and the Asian territories of the British Empire were demanding it. Black Africa was still the dark continent with all its history before it.

## II

### The New Partition of Africa

WHEN I speak of the partition of Africa I am thinking of Africa not as a geographical but as an ethnological expression. The north coast of Africa as far back as the watershed of the Atlas range is part of the Mediterranean basin, inhabited throughout history by peoples of the same racial type as live in the other Mediterranean states enjoying a similar climate. The extreme southern tip of Africa, the Cape of Good Hope and its neighbouring region, is also distinguished from the hinterland by a temperate climate and characteristic flora. The Cape, so far as we know, had never been occupied by any settled population until the Dutch colonized it in the seventeenth century. The problems of North Africa and of South Africa are essentially frontier problems, such as the determination of the reasonable and legitimate limits of white settlement. The Africans, as the word is usually understood—that is to say, the Negro peoples—have never been indigenous either on the Mediterranean coast or near the Cape of Good Hope, and, therefore, when speaking of the partition of Africa, I exclude those regions from my discussion.

Africa proper has a very short history. A hundred years

ago even the general pattern of its geography was unknown, and within living memory there were vast blank
spaces on the map in which the land of *Prester John* or
*King Solomon's Mines* might yet be found. Though the
whole coastline of the continent was familiar to European
traders, few had penetrated the interior of even the coastal
colonies which had long been under European control.
The first partition of Africa was made as recently as in the
score of years between 1884 and 1904, and followed hard
upon Stanley's exploration of the Congo, which for the
first time elucidated the geographical pattern of the
interior. The true relationship between the river systems
of the Nile, Niger, and Congo was revealed, with the
consequence that penetration of the heart of Africa became
possible. What were the motives of the men who searched
for the sources of the African rivers? James Bruce, Mungo
Park, Speke, and Stanley were fired with the pure desire
for knowledge; to them the exploration of the unknown
was a task that needed no justification. The partition of
Africa took place at that time and in that way because it
followed, inevitably as we may suppose, from the scientific
drive for the exploration of the world which was so marked
a feature of the nineteenth century. Why our ancestors
were content for centuries to live in the Old World without discovering the New, and why in the sixteenth century
they remedied this default, is too large a subject to inves-
tigate here. Certainly, the whole pattern of world affairs
was changed by the exploration and partition of the
Americas. Similarly, the pattern of our world to-day is
being changed by the exploration and partition of Africa.
The urge to expansion has a technological side and a
psychological side, but in the original impulse there was

almost no economic motive. Mungo Park on the Niger,
Speke at the source of the Nile, and Stanley on his first
visit to the Congo were not at all influenced by the pres-
sures of trade and finance. The impulsion of capital was
first felt at a much later stage. In 1857 Dr Livingstone
returned to Britain after his exploration of the Zambesi
and was lionized by the people and the Government. He
electrified the country by an address before the University
of Cambridge. "I direct your attention to Africa," he said.
"I go back to Africa to try to make an open path for commerce and Christianity. Do you carry out the work which
I have begun."[1] Five years later the news that Speke had
discovered the source of the Nile and had thus solved the
puzzle that had defied geographers for near three thousand
years was flashed back to London by the new telegraph in
four words: "The Nile is settled."[2] All Europe was fired
with enthusiasm for African exploration, so that before
long forty-five separate exploring expeditions were afield
at once in various parts of tropical Africa. Marchand's
crossing of the continent from the Congo to the Nile and
his historic meeting with Kitchener at Fashoda in 1898
marked the end of the heroic age of African travel.

The name of Livingstone and his plea for commerce and
Christianity brings us to the next factor in the sum. If
science and adventure, and the love of exploring the
unknown provided the first motive; the second was provided by philanthropy. And now we must face the hideous
story of the carrying trade in slaves from Africa to
America, a staple of British shipping for about a hundred
years. As far back as history records, African rulers have
grown rich by preying upon one another and selling their
captives into slavery. The rulers of Egypt from the

C

nineteenth century B.C. to the nineteenth century A.D. have
had a particularly bad name for this deplorable trade, but it
was most highly commercialized on the coastal strip of
West Africa where many local potentates built up powerful organizations for catching and selling men. Bargaining
was stiff, since West Africans are born traders, and com-
petition was fierce among buyers. The European merchants
broke into this trade as middlemen, and, owing to their
superior naval and shipping strength, the British dominated it from 1713 to 1806. It paid them best, of course, to
deliver the goods—live human beings—to the American
buyers in strong and healthy condition. Having come late
into the business and done very well out of it, the British
did what no one else had ever done before: they repented
of it. They abolished the trade at great financial loss to
themselves and, for more than fifty years, employed one-
sixth of the Royal Navy, in war as well as in peace, in
suppressing the slave trade wherever it appeared.

During the seventeenth and eighteenth centuries most
of the European Powers had established footholds on the
West African coast by virtue of treaties with African
chiefs and had built forts to protect their slave-trading
posts. The Gold Coast to this day is studded with old
ruined castles, some of them, like Christiansborg, now the
residence of Dr Nkrumah, handsome examples of Renais-
sance architecture. When the slave trade was abolished,
some European Powers withdrew from Africa and others
sold their interests to the British, who remained to play a
reversed role. Formerly their installations had been maintained to promote the lucrative trade in slaves. Now they
were preserved for the unprofitable task of suppressing
that trade.

From the abolition of the slave trade until the end of
the nineteenth century big business in Britain was quite
remarkably uninterested in Africa. The impulse to expansion, to the extension of Empire, came almost exclusively
from philanthropists. Missionaries persuaded Gladstone
to set up the first protectorate at the mouth of the Niger,
drew what Rhodes called the imperial factor into Bechuanaland, and involved the British in Uganda. The great
hero of Britain in Africa during the 1850s, 1860s, and
1870s was Dr Livingstone. To this day, if you leave the
main roads, the commercial cities down on the coast, and
the administrative centres in Africa, and go into the bush,
the first and often the only mark of Western civilization is
the mission station. The Christian missionary societies are
still the channels through which Western ideals and Western technology first find their way into the minds of
primitive Africans. Even in such advanced states as Ghana
more than half of all education is still in the hands of the
missionaries; in states like Tanganyika the figure is more
than eighty per cent. These remarks do not apply only
to British colonial Africa. They are hardly less true of
French Africa and perhaps more true of Belgian Africa.
But statistics of missionary effort are woefully scanty.

In 1865 a parliamentary committee sat in London to
discuss the future of British West African settlements now
that the slave trade was suppressed on that coast. It recommended that Britain should withdraw altogether from
West Africa except from Sierra Leone, the settlement for
freed slaves.[3] In 1885, after the Berlin West African Conference, a Liberal Government, over which Mr Gladstone
presided, staked out a claim to a sphere of influence on the
Niger which has grown in the course of seventy years to

be the great federal state of Nigeria, now enjoying independence—a state nearly twice as large as Texas and with three times the population. No historian has as yet given a satisfactory answer to the question why Britain, France, Belgium, and Germany, all of which were trying to keep clear of tropical Africa in the 1860s and 1870s, greedily divided it among themselves in the 1880s and 1890s. There is a standard explanation, sedulously propagated by the communists, that the machinations of high finance will account for all. Surplus capital seeking a new outlet, according to orthodox anti-imperialists, provided the motive force. A mere glance at the facts of economic history will reveal that this explanation is wholly unsatisfactory, and that with it the whole myth of imperialist exploitation collapses.[4] Tropical Africa has always been and still is desperately short of capital, and the adventurers who conducted the partition, whatever their true motives, alike failed to interest capitalists in their enterprises. The 1880s were a period of economic recession when unusually little European capital was available for export. What there was went mostly to Australia and the Argentine, where there were much safer investments. Big business in Paris was certainly *not* interested in the Sahara Desert; big business in London was *not* interested in the Nigerian uplands. Neither of these regions produced much that London or Paris wanted to buy.

The forces that brought pressure on the European governments were the missionaries, who wished to evangelize Africa; their philanthropic supporters, who were determined to suppress the internal slave trade as they had suppressed the external slave trade; and the practical men, who judged, quite rightly, that Africa could be civilized only by the growth of trade under settled administrations. Commerce and Christianity, Livingstone's formula, was the programme for Africa. But trade was still a very small affair, not enough to raise a flutter on the stock market.

In 1884 the growing concern with Africa was touched off by the conference which Bismarck summoned at Berlin. He was not himself much attracted to colonial expansion, and though Germany came in for some pickings they were not his primary objective. Bismarck's intention was to embroil France and Britain with one another in Africa in order to distract them from combining against him in Europe. In this diplomatic intrigue he failed, and the final result of his endeavours was a peaceful partition between Britain and France of all the unadministered region of Central Africa. This was completed in three main stages, in 1890, 1898, and 1904; the last being the settlement of outstanding disputes called the Entente Cordiale.[5]

But this was not the most important result of the Berlin West African Conference. From its deliberations was derived the series of international instruments (commonly called the Congo treaties, though they are applied to regions far wider than the Congo Basin), which have regulated the action of the European Powers in tropical Africa for more than seventy years. As revised by the Convention of St Germain after the First World War they are still operative, and are likely to be much discussed when the implications of admitting African territories to the European Economic Community come up for examination.[6]

Broadly speaking, the Congo treaties were designed to establish the whole of tropical Africa as a free trade area from which the slave trade, the arms trade, and the liquor trade were to be excluded. Subsequent failure to carry out the whole programme does not detract from the grandeur of the original design. In short, the terms of the partition of Africa between the signatories to the Congo treaties was far above the average moral standard of international affairs in the nineteenth century.

The exploitation of Africa was now afoot, and again I must emphasize how short has been the time in which so much has been accomplished. The conquest of tropical disease began only with Ross's identification of the malarial mosquito in 1897; the opening of the East African interior only with the building of the Uganda railway in 1902; the linking of northern and southern Nigeria dates only from 1912; the first autonomous universities only from 1948. Before the First World War little more than pioneering work was done: the creation of administrative systems, the imposition of law and order. It was only between the wars that Africa began to prosper.

Few tasks are harder for the student than to recapture the mood of thirty or forty years ago, the phase of history which has receded from personal memory but has not yet been revised and rationalized by the historians. Every generation revolts against the preceding one by dis- counting the reminiscences of old men who, it is supposed, idealize the conditions of their youth. We must now attempt to recall a period when the great majority of British people had no misgivings about the Empire, when loyalty to the imperial tradition was, on the whole, more fervent in the colonies than in the mother country, when Asian and African magnates vied with one another in protesting their loyalty to the Crown, when an Indian philanthropist endowed the Imperial Institute in London,

when the Malay States presented a battleship to the Royal
Navy. So thoroughly has the word imperialism been
smeared by the followers of Hobson and Lenin that some
effort is required to recall a time when most conservatives
and many liberals took pride in being imperialists, when
even the Fabian Society, which contributed so much to
socialist thinking, came down decidedly in favour of an
enlightened imperial policy.[7] The Fabians were talking of
the change from Empire to Commonwealth many years
before Lionel Curtis and his Round Table group popular-
ized the term. Little Englanders there have always been,
the political heirs of the radicals who had opposed the
American War, but I cannot recall that they ever formed
a government or constituted an official opposition in the
nineteenth or early twentieth centuries. When John Bright
opposed Canadian confederation in 1867, on the grounds
that it would postpone the desirable day of Canadian
secession from the Empire, he spoke for himself alone.
When Lloyd George opposed the South African War in
1899 he did not carry the Liberal Party with him and,
what is more remarkable, he failed to enlist the support of
any of the self-governing colonies who, on the contrary,
rallied to the imperial cause.[8] It was in the 1920s that
anti-imperialism was put forward as a constructive principle by effective and organized political parties, and that
the first crisis concerning imperialism arose in British
India.

When the British people thought about their Empire
thirty or forty years ago they thought first of the white
Dominions and secondly of India. Though they did not
very well understand the metaphysical subtlety of the
Balfour formula, they were fully aware of what Dominion

status meant in practice, and were proud that the four original Dominions had attained to it. There were few in Great Britain who did not nourish the hope that a formula had been found to solve the age-long Irish problem. But I fear that this general agreement was of the kind that John Stuart Mill called the "deep slumber of a decided opinion."[9] It was taken for granted and not much thought about.

On the future of India, however, there was a very marked cleavage of opinion, and it did not follow party lines. It would be somewhat nearer the truth to say that the intelligentsia of all parties in Britain addressed themselves to Indian affairs in the belief that India must soon proceed to responsible self-government within the Empire. That at least was the intention stated in the Montagu-Chelmsford Report of 1917, and in the Government of India Act of 1935,[10] both of which were sponsored by coalition governments with a majority of Conservative supporters. Optimists then thought that in time these measures would lead a united India down the well-trodden path to Dominion status, and idealists may yet deplore the failure to achieve that goal. But my classification of the supporters of this measure as the intelligentsia is again insufficient unless I exclude from that category Sir Winston Churchill and others who opposed the practical steps taken towards Indian self-government as premature and dangerous.[11] This scepticism was by no means confined to the governing class. A canvas of British working-class voters would very probably have found a majority for firm government in India in 1936, just as twenty years later, in the opinion of many good judges, they were for strong action at Suez.

Why did the Government of India Act fail? The rising tide of nationalism had brought back the panacea, self-determination; the political leaders in India were set upon solving their problems in their own way; and the fatal British error was the London Conference of 1930 where the plan for an Indian Constitution was drawn up by a panel of British experts. The Indian National Congress, which once had been a docile body, opening its proceedings with a loyal address to the Crown, had now become something quite different—a shadow government with an alternative plan. The enlightened Indian leaders, the natural co-operators, to whom the transfer of power must eventually be made, had committed themselves to non-co-operation, and the cause of gradual progress to Dominion status was lost.

Discussions about the Empire in the 1920s, unless about Ireland and India, turned most frequently towards the settler colonies in the eastern half of Africa. It was assumed that one could be optimistic about the future, since the generous-hearted Smuts towered over his Afrikaner colleagues and rivals. So eminent a philosopher and statesman might be trusted to disentangle the confusion into which the Union of South Africa had repeatedly lapsed in the previous century. "History," he had said, "writes the word, Reconciliation, over all her quarrels."[12] Adopting the same view, the British Government gently pushed Rhodesia in the direction of joining the Union of South Africa.[13]

We can find in British colonial history only one obvious example to support the Hobsonian hypothesis that the impulse towards imperialism stems from the need of outlets for surplus capital. That is the early colonization of

Rhodesia, which the directors of the Chartered Company launched expressly as a speculation. It turned out to be a bad speculation which paid no dividends at all for thirty years. The just complaint against Rhodes is not that he exploited Central Africa to grow rich but that he induced investors in London to back his political fancy in the mistaken expectation that they might grow rich. On his own account he had acquired wealth in order to appropriate Central Africa and he squandered his wealth on developing it. The shareholders in London found little profit in Rhodes's dream and certainly no quick returns, and the settlers who went to Rhodesia protested loudly against the privileges of the Chartered Company. Like all other settlers in every British colony before and since, they clamoured for self-government. Forty years ago self-government did not yet mean thoroughgoing democracy with universal suffrage. That new-fangled device was enjoyed by Australia and New Zealand but by few other countries in the world, not by Britain itself before 1918 and even then with qualifications. If Cape Colony had self-government with a limited franchise which admitted only a fortunate few among the coloured race, why should not Rhodesia have a similar system? In the discussions about responsible government for Rhodesia it is an astonishing fact that the colour bar was rarely mentioned. Votes for the African masses were not discussed, not claimed, and apparently not wanted; the question simply did not arise. The two vital problems in Rhodesia were the appropriation of land, and relations with the Union of South Africa.

The question of the ownership of land in Rhodesia was a crucial issue in Imperial history. Since the eighteenth century a distinction had been drawn between colonies of settlement, where the English common law is assumed to grow from the soil, with a consequent right of every settler to a vote, and colonies by conquest or cession, in which the Crown had an absolute right to legislate by Order-in-Council.[14]

What was the precise status of the Chartered Company in a colony approaching self-government? And, especially, what rights did it command over unappropriated land, the future wealth of Rhodesia?

This question came before the Privy Council just at the time of the outbreak of the First World War, which delayed the proceedings so long that the War was drawing to a close when Lord Sumner, on July 29, 1918, delivered a momentous judgment.[15] The Company claimed rights over the land by virtue of their treaties with the Matabele king; the Privy Council refuted this claim on the grounds that King Lobengula had been overthrown in war. Rhodesia was thus a colony by conquest and its unalienated lands were the property of the Crown. The Sumner judgment had made it plain that the land and the administration went together. If the Company forfeited one it must forfeit the other, and the way was cleared for the settlers to demand some such measure of self-government as earlier British colonies had enjoyed.

The Colonial Office, over which Sir Winston Churchill then presided, made it clear to the settlers' leaders that the Union of South Africa was now to be completed by a Rhodesian province running as far north as the Zambesi; but, rather to the surprise of Whitehall and Pretoria, the Rhodesian settlers voted for autonomous status as a self-governing colony. They knew their neighbours well enough and were not disposed to submit to Afrikaner domination. The plebiscite in which they voted for responsible government by 9000 votes to 6000—so small a community were they—was held in 1922, and Southern Rhodesia has practised the art of self-government for more than a whole generation.[16]

The granting of self-government to Britain's colonies has always been a constructive process; not only is it contrary to precedent[17] for a British Government to withdraw a measure of freedom given to a colony, but an Act of Parliament is required to do so, and an Act cannot be passed without a political struggle in the House of Commons. A self-governing colony is likely to resist any effort to restrict its powers, and, furthermore, inevitably enlarges those powers by dealing with new problems as they arise, and by creating new precedents which Whitehall has no inclination to question. Self-government is an ever-growing function, and critics of Rhodesian policy to-day may tend to overlook the distinction between the nominal and real authority of the British Government, which cannot now begin to resume a legal authority that has been atrophying for thirty years. Nor can the status of Southern Rhodesia be defined in terms of new Commonwealth principles; the territory attained to responsible government before the Statute of Westminster and before the Balfour formula was devised, and does not rely upon them for its sanction. With Newfoundland and India, Southern Rhodesia was represented at the Ottawa Conference of 1932; with Burma it sent its premier as an observer to the Imperial Conference of 1937.

It fell to the new government of Rhodesia to devise a system of allotting rights over the land. Large tracts had been appropriated and granted to settlers as early as 1894, and a general settlement of the land had been attempted by the Chartered Company between 1914 and 1920, with the consequence that the unalienated land to which the Sumner judgment referred was but a fraction of the whole. The settlement made under the Rhodesian Land Apportionment Act of 1930 was therefore restricted in scope by past alienations, notably by the confiscation of tribal land after the Matabele war. The only excuse to be made for these discreditable seizures is that land shortage was not the problem that it was in other parts of Africa. The whole population numbered less than four persons to the square mile. However, here is a good example of imperialism in practice, a repetition of the way in which Normans expropriated Saxons in England, Europeans expropriated Indians in Kentucky, and the Matabele themselves had expropriated the Mashona only forty years before the coming of Rhodes's pioneers. Out of a total of 96 million acres in Southern Rhodesia, 47 million were allotted for white settlement, 31 million were reserved for Africans, and 18 million were held unassigned. Before commenting on these facts let us turn to Kenya, where, in the same years, a very different train of events may be observed.

The Conservative Government which had transferred power in Rhodesia rather roughly refused to do the same in Kenya, another settler-colony on a still smaller scale. Here too land-tenure was at the heart of the matter. White settlers had begun to move to Kenya early in the century precisely because it was empty country with a temperate climate. All the early travellers[18] agreed in stating that the district now called the White Highlands was lying waste and unappropriated, though there is some justification for the counter-claim that it was temporarily abandoned on account of cattle plagues and tribal wars. Whether or no, the migration of British settlers into the Kenya highlands since 1903 marks the last phase in the three-hundred-year-old history of emigration from Britain, which began with Raleigh's expedition and which has peopled almost all the unoccupied lands of the temperate zones with settlers of Anglo-Saxon stock. The end of the colonizing age was marked by the scrupulous restrictions imposed upon the Kenya settlers by a Colonial Office which had become aware of a changing world.

How can we account for the different policies pursued in Kenya and Rhodesia? Partly they differed because the tribal system had been broken in Rhodesia, because the settlers had been established for a generation, and because Rhodesia was conceived of as a natural extension of the Union of South Africa. But there was another reason. In the coastal ports of East Africa and in the townships along the new East African railway, trade was in the hands of Indian merchants who had been established there before the European settlers. The railway had been built by imported Indian labourers who had stayed in the country. It was the Indian interest in East Africa that procured its special treatment in Whitehall. If the Indian Congress leaders had shown more concern for their compatriots in East Africa the country might have become a dependency of the British Indian Empire, as the Kenya Indians wished, instead of becoming a British colony. But the white settlers, who were paternally disposed towards the Africans, were bitterly hostile to the Indians, their rivals in the development of the country, and it was to exclude the Indians that they campaigned for white self-government and a white reservation in the Kenya highlands. It is a curious comment on imperial policy that in the frequent parliamentary debates on East Africa during the 1920s the issue was not at first between the conflicting claims of Europeans and Africans but between the conflicting claims of Europeans and Asians. After several exchanges, which in one instance produced a threat of rebellion among the white settlers, a decision was given in 1923 by the Duke of Devonshire (who had succeeded Winston Churchill at the Colonial Office) in the document remembered simply as the Kenya White Paper. "Kenya is an African territory," he said, "and the interests of the African natives must be paramount, and if the interests of the immigrant races should conflict . . . the former should prevail."[19]

This being the fundamental principle, concessions were made to the immigrants: the white settlers were to keep their highland area intact, and the Asians were to have separate representation in the Legislative Council on a communal roll. Grudgingly the white settlers accepted the decision, but the Asians, thus condemned to be second-class citizens, broke out into protest. Their forum was the House of Lords, where two former viceroys of different parties combined to champion the cause of the Indian colonists, pointing out that Lord Reading, the viceroy then in office, had publicly denounced the Kenya White Paper in India. The rival ambitions of British and Indian settlers[20] were both condemned by Parliament and the doctrine of the White Paper stood unamended until 1959.

The year 1923 was thus crucial in African history: it marked the close of Smuts's regime in South Africa, the granting of self-government in Rhodesia, and the refusal of self-government in Kenya. In each of these great territories the allotment of land was a more serious issue than the franchise, and a simple table will distinguish the problems of the three countries.[21]

|  | Proportion of Europeans to Whole Population | Proportion of Land Allotted for European Use |
|---|---|---|
| South Africa | 21.0 per cent. | 89 per cent. |
| Southern Rhodesia | 8.4 per cent. | 49 per cent. |
| Kenya | 1.2 per cent. | 7 per cent. |

While public attention, so far as it was ever given to colonial Africa, was focused upon the settler-colonies in the east, another empire had arisen, almost unnoticed, in the west. Those who cared began to hear talk in the later 1920s of two distinct policies—one for the east coast and another for the west coast. On the east side progress was conceived in terms of raising the productivity of the country by planting European settlers in suitable patches, to grow an export crop, to create trade and revenue, and to set an example of high farming which the tribesmen would eventually learn to imitate. This was the policy inherited from enlightened colonial governors of the last century. Administration, a simpler version of the British-Indian system, meant little more than keeping law and order and collecting some kind of direct tax, usually a hut tax which barely repaid the cost of administration. But in West Africa, traditionally the white man's grave, there were no settlers, only merchants—significantly called "palm-oil ruffians"—who bargained in pidgin-English for the oil-seeds that Europe was beginning to demand in quantity. Three factors made up the sum of British imperialism in West Africa. The traders pushed their buying agencies deeper into the interior and especially up the channels of the Niger; the missionaries urged the Government to step in and control barbarous African chiefs and corrupt European traders; and the Government intervened, not because it wanted the expense and trouble of administration, but because not to do so would have given the advantage to a rival power. The Scottish missionaries at Calabar persuaded Gladstone to set up the Oil Rivers Protectorate at the mouth of the Niger; the tiny National Africa Company, one of the progenitors of the Unilever combine, engrossed the trade of the Middle Niger after buying out its French competitors; and the manœuvrings at the Berlin West African Conference of 1885 swung the whole region into the British rather than the French sphere of influence.[22] Gladstone was willing to leave all to the traders and the missionaries, and in his day the Royal Niger Company exercised all the colonial government there was. It was during Chamberlain's great administration that the Colonial Office decided to give Frederick Lugard the authority to found a nation-state. Between 1893 and 1903 the partition of Africa was completed and the competitive advances of French and British empire-builders into the heart of the continent took the form of campaigns against the last slave-raiding kingdoms, north of the Niger, around Lake Chad, in the Sudan, and far away in Nyasaland.

When Lugard, with no money and a handful of white assistants, subdued the great Moslem emirates of what is now the Northern Region of Nigeria, he could neither administer nor develop the country. He could merely pacify it and wait for beneficent commerce to bring progress. His celebrated invention of indirect rule—ruling by taking over the traditional native system—was a matter of

D

necessity, not of choice. Here were the emirates with their Islamic laws and systems, and if they could be prevented from preying on their neighbours it was all that could be done for the present.

The great expanses of territory in the British spheres of influence were acquired by treaties between native rulers and British consular officers who derived their authority from the Foreign Jurisdictions Act.[23] The need to impose extraterritorial jurisdiction on British subjects in lands where there was no regular government, and the need to protect them from oppression by barbarous rulers, induced British governments to invoke the provisions of this Act, which gave consular officers a limited jurisdiction over their own nationals. Gradually these officials in the wilder parts of the earth began to intervene in tribal politics, and they became advisers and protectors of tribal rulers. There were many instances in which petty chiefs were persuaded, for a consideration, to put their mark upon documents they hardly pretended to understand. But nineteenth-century history also records a number of explicit, negotiated treaties in which emergent native peoples willingly—indeed, enthusiastically—placed themselves under British protection in order to gain access to the trade and culture of the Western world.

There is nothing in the history of the Treaty of Waitangi made with the New Zealand chiefs in 1840, the Bond Treaty with the Gold Coast chiefs in 1844, the Basutoland Treaty of 1868, or the Buganda Agreement of 1900 which both parties need not recall with pride. The relation between the protecting power and the tribal government was, in the first instance, diplomatic; the British Government dealt with the external relations of the protectorate through the Foreign Office and interfered with their internal affairs as little as possible. A protectorate was held to be in a very satisfactory state if it was quiet, orderly, and self-supporting.

To appreciate this attitude, we must try to understand the political climate of a world where *laisser-faire* was the accepted rule of government. There was as yet no suggestion of the welfare state and no hint or notion that a dynamic development policy was the duty of the government even in Britain. In Africa, commerce and Christianity, the trader and the missionary, were held responsible for social progress. Perhaps the first administration in the British Empire to plan economic development on a large scale was the Government of the Punjab with its policy of irrigation and land settlement. Perhaps the most enlightened of all governments in any British dependency was that in the Sudan, which was administered from the Foreign Office instead of the Colonial Office. The first comprehensive effort to convert the miscellaneous mass of protectorates and colonies into political units that could enter the civilized world, that could be (to use our modern phrase) viable, was made when Joseph Chamberlain was at the Colonial Office, from 1895 to 1902. He took over a number of territories administered either by chartered companies or as protectorates under the Foreign Office, bringing them within the scope of his colonial policy. He established the first technical services in health and agriculture, and he began to open up backward areas with railways. Now, at last, the regeneration of Africa began. It was the Uganda Railway that opened East Africa, and it was the line inland from Lagos (it did not reach Kano until 1912) that first made the concept of a Nigerian state a possibility. Neither the name, the entity, nor the idea of a nation had previously existed.

In all these countries money was desperately lacking. Surplus capital seeking an outlet went anywhere rather than to the newly acquired empire in tropical Africa, so that all progress was made on the cheap. Lugard's system of indirect rule proved to be the only practicable policy, and was adapted to the needs of other colonial regions where social life was not as well-organized as in Islamic northern Nigeria. It became a cult and was much favoured by the practitioners of a new-fangled science called anthropology. In its extremest form indirect rule was described or parodied as the 'zoological gardens policy:'[24] "Leave the simple savages alone and do not allow them to be corrupted by the sophistications of the West." But Africa itself had a comment to make on this point of view. The African tribesmen were not so simple, and most of those who had sufficient knowledge of the outside world to consider the alternatives were determined to move with the times. There were exceptions: tribes such as the Masai of Kenya stubbornly refused to modify their traditional customs. But, by and large, the Africans could see for themselves that the white man's magic was more powerful than their own and they studied to master it.

The method of indirect rule in British tropical Africa was to establish 'native authorities' based upon the tribal organization. The dominant factor was always land-tenure and the West African policy intended that the land should not be alienated. There were too many parts of the world, Southern Rhodesia, Swaziland, Fiji (not to mention earlier examples in America), where recognition of tribal authority had merely enabled the tribal chiefs to sell the land to

concession-hunters. Under the Lugard system the aliena-
tion of land was prevented. An interesting case in colonial
history is the sustained attempt of Unilever (in one of its
earlier forms) to acquire land in West Africa in order to
create a plantation economy like that which one of its
subsidiaries had set up in French Africa, or like that
which the American Firestone Company had set up in
Liberia.[25] The Colonial Office stood firm and the system
of British West African agriculture to this day is based
on peasant-culture not on plantation-culture. The West
Africans were far more advanced socially than the East
Africans; they had very clear notions of producing an
export crop and of selling it to the best advantage. The
market is the centre of life in West Africa where every
man and woman is a born trader.

The first great step forward was taken in the Gold
Coast (not then known as Ghana) when an enterprising
governor, Sir Gordon Guggisberg (1919-27) took advantage of the boom in cocoa to initiate a development policy.
He built a new harbour at Takoradi on that harbourless
coast, and he devised an educational system upon the
advice of James Aggrey, whose name should be honoured
as the first Ghanaian to move into the modern world.
Cocoa, recently introduced to West Africa by the British,
was grown by the peasants on their own holdings, and was
sold through middlemen to the external trading companies,
of which the United African Company, a Unilever constituent, was the chief.

The Gold Coast people demonstrated their modernity
in 1937 by a cocoa-growers' strike, which compelled the
buyers to give them better terms. A further consequence
of this prosperity was the capital for the rapid development

that enabled Ghana, first of African colonies, to proceed to full self-government.

Education is the key to all progress. In the trading communities of the West African seaports there has long been an educated African middle class, few in numbers but influential, which has no counterpart on the east side of Africa. Wherever there are Christian missions there are schools, and as long ago as 1875 the missionary college at Fourah Bay, in Sierra Leone, became associated with the English University of Durham, so that Sierra Leone boys took Arts degrees and became the intellectual aristocracy of the Coast. Law students and medical students from West Africa found their way to London or to the Scottish universities, where, since they were British subjects, no one was concerned to count their numbers or to supervise their welfare any more than to count or supervise British subjects of another colour. England itself had no comprehensive scheme of general education at all levels until 1918, and it was only after a commission of inquiry, sponsored by American philanthropy, that the Colonial Office applied itself to the problem of educating Africa. The limiting factor was shortage of money and the method of applying what money was available was the same as in England. Colonial governments did not set up state systems of education, which they could not afford, but subsidized the existing voluntary schools, that is, the mission schools. The District Officers, the real old Africa hands, and even the missionaries, favoured education in the vernacular since that was the way to reach the unsophisticated masses. The middle-class Africans pressed for the English language which they saw as the outlet to a wider world. Only by taking the same examinations as the English boy could they be sure of attaining to equality with him. Just before the Second World War the cause of colonial education was much publicized, and at that time the impetus for a great move forward came from another colonial region.

Unrest in the West Indies in the 1930s had led to the appointment of a commission which took the bold step of proposing long-term planning for development and welfare. Just then war broke out, and the report of the commission was not published in full; but the leaven that had long been working in the Colonial Office was not smothered by wartime distractions; and at a great crisis in history Neville Chamberlain's Government introduced a Bill that was worthy of the son of Joseph Chamberlain. The Colonial Development and Welfare Act, designed to finance locally devised plans of progress in each colony, was debated calmly and confidently in the House of Commons in May 1940 when the British Army was falling back on Dunkirk and the faint-hearted in other countries assumed that Britain and her colonies were perishing together.[26]

Long overdue, as we may now think, the scheme was in tune with the spirit of the age. The world had been shaken by the great depression and had emerged from it convinced that *laisser-faire* was not an adequate policy. The new dynamic was to be applied in home and colonial affairs together. After the war there would be no return to the age of retrenchment. About this time a new word began to be bandied about in colonial circles, the word 'expatriates.' In the old days men and women who went to an under-developed country as administrators, technicians, or teachers, constituted a ruling class with an unquestioned status. The fall of Singapore and the quit-India campaign put an end to all that. Colonialists were now recognized as temporary visitors who remained in the country on sufferance, even if the work they were doing was appreciated. It was overlooked that there were African expatriates in Britain and America as well as British expatriates in Africa. A quarter of a million African soldiers served outside their own territories in the Second World War, very many of them in South-east Asia, where they saw for themselves the downfall of the colonial empires, a lesson not likely to be forgotten.

An even more influential group of African expatriates were the wandering scholars who made their way to universities in the advanced countries. Dr Nkrumah, Dr Azikiwe, Dr Banda, Mr Mboya, Mr Nyerere, and their fellows in French Africa are the products of European and American, not of African, culture. The theories they hold and the policies they promote are imported, just as foreign in their origin as the notions and policies of the colonial administrators. Moreover, these national leaders are expatriates in their ways of thinking. In earlier days, a full measure of education could be attained by an African only if he made his way to a university overseas. The immense majority of such fortunate students from British Africa went to Britain. The Colonial Development and Welfare Act of 1940 gave serious thought to expatriation in higher education. The very able report of a Royal Commission in 1945[27] declared positively that the colonies could attain real self-government only if they had national systems of education; that a state that sent its best scholars to London for an expatriate education was in no real sense independent; and that a chain of universities for the colonies was essential to their development plans. Accordingly, four new universities have been founded in British colonial

Africa (chiefly at the cost of the British taxpayer), and two in other colonies. Several more will soon appear. Admirable as is the progress of these institutions, it has not yet been sufficient to form the character of the educated class in the colonies. There are no short cuts to higher education, and until several generations have passed through the new universities the national leaders will still be the expatriates. The Pan-African movement, of which more will be heard in the coming years, did not originate in Africa but among expatriates in America, some of them expatriates by several generations who had never themselves set foot in Africa.

I can find little evidence that anyone in British or French Africa, black or white, foresaw in the 1930s the outburst of democratic activity that was to convulse Africa in the 1940s. Let us look for a moment at French Africa where the colonial policy was, perhaps, more advanced than in the British territories, and where the beginnings of political agitation were less evident. In French Africa the policy and the code of administration had a history of more than a hundred years. The intention was to create a French-African *élite* with full French citizenship, so as to bind the colonies and the metropolis together under a uniform system. In Senegal this magnanimous project already had a long history, but in other territories, as in British Africa, time had been too short to do more than make a beginning. On the whole, the centralized administration and the vigorous educational system, which sent every good scholar to complete his training in France, seemed to be effective. Educated French Africans were more ready to become Frenchmen than British Africans to become Englishmen, but then the British has no such intention. So far as they had a policy it was colonial nationalism in the far future, like that of Canada. The result, as summed up by one good observer was: "In British West Africa everyone who is politically conscious is a nationalist of some kind. In French West Africa there are Catholics and anti-clericals, Communists and Gaullists, Socialists, Syndicalists, and Existentialists."[28]

Although this tranquil period of development on the French side had its counterpart on the British side in the period of indirect rule, the eruption of modern political notions occurred a few years earlier in British Africa. It is now a curious experience to look back at the classical volumes on African development written between the wars. Such enlightened and forward-looking studies as Lugard's *The Dual Mandate in British Tropical Africa* (1922) or even Lord Hailey's first edition of *An African Survey* (1938) are concerned with the west coast policy and its possible extension to other parts of Africa, with the improvement of peasant cultivation, the organization of marketing, the building up of an educational system, and, in general, with the development of native leadership. African self-consciousness was hardly yet a factor in the situation, but a closer study of Lord Hailey's wise pronouncements reveals a note of warning that the native authorities were not enough:

> In many areas the system [of indirect rule through native authorities] has been far more successful than the procedure of native administration formerly in use; but its real test will come when the traditional native authorities are faced with the necessity of introducing social services on something more than the rudimentary scale to which they are now accustomed. It will be subject to a further test with the

growth of political and national aspirations in Africa. . . . Up to the present time the fact that the system makes little provision for recognizing educated opinion has not resulted in open opposition to it; in the future, however, it will inevitably have to meet pressure due to this cause. . . . One of the gravest problems will be the development of a legal and administrative system which will provide for the rapidly growing class whose social life is not assimilated to that of the Europeans but which cannot be suitably regulated by tribal institutions.[29]

After the Second World War there was no problem of reconquest or liberation in British Africa as there was in British Asia. Throughout the war the colonial regimes persisted and, on the whole, the primary producers in the colonies prospered. Nevertheless, the post-War reconstruction revealed a psychological revolution. The slow pace of colonial development would no longer serve; new means of communication by Press and radio were reaching out towards the hitherto untouched tribesmen and, most important of all, the leadership of African opinion was passing from the chiefs to the professional politicians from the towns with their expatriate education. The chiefs might still control the tribal lands of which they were the traditional guardians; the new politicians had their roots in the trade unions which spread with the beginnings of industrialism.

The psychological revolution was not confined to the colonies; it also took place at Whitehall and Westminster. The general line of policy favoured by the Colonial Office before the Second World War was expressed by a senior official in these words:

While there is no such thing as a typical Crown Colony Government, it is possible to trace in the Colonial Empire

a series of stages in development, from a benevolent auto-
cracy towards a progressive association of the inhabitants of
the various dependencies with the control of their own
affairs. Development along these lines . . . is not likely to
follow any uniform pattern. It must be adapted to the needs
and circumstances of the various countries ; here it may
take the form of parliamentary institutions, there that of the
independent growth of indigenous states within what is now
a single administration.[30]

By 1942 opinion had grown firmer: "We are pledged,"
said the Secretary of State for the Colonies, "to guide
Colonial peoples along the road to self-government
within the framework of the British Empire."[31] This was
more specific in intention than the undertaking given by
the colonial Powers in the United Nations Charter three
years later. What they then agreed was "to take due
account of the political aspirations of the peoples, and to
assist them in the progressive development of their free
political institutions, according to the particular circumstances of each territory and its peoples, and their varying
stages of advancement."[32]

It fell to the Labour Government in Britain, especially
while Mr A. Creech Jones was Colonial Secretary (1946-
1950), to apply these principles during the post-War
reconstruction. Though much credit for the practical
measures must accrue to him, it is to be shared with his
unnamed advisers and assistants in the Colonial Office.
There was little perceptible change in the general policy
when the Conservatives returned to power. The most con-
cise statement of the object of both parties was made by
Mr Oliver Lyttelton in 1951:

Certain broad lines of policy are accepted by all sections of
the House as being above party politics. . . . First we all aim

at helping the colonial territories to attain self-government within the British Commonwealth. Secondly we are determined to pursue the economic and social development of the colonial territories so that it keeps pace with their political development.[33]

In economic planning there was one strange aberration during the post-War period which should be mentioned if only because of its unusual character in British colonial history. The Tanganyika Groundnuts Scheme, on which upward of £30 millions was squandered, provided no direct advantage either to the peoples of the territory or to the Commonwealth as a whole. The deviation from traditional policy lay in the object of the scheme; it was designed primarily to provide cheap food for the people of Britain and only secondarily to develop a backward part of Africa.[34] The primary objective was never reached, and the Africans who were to have enjoyed the secondary advantages did not get them in the form that was intended. But this blind alley in colonial development is now only of historical interest.

The rapid and accelerating moves towards political independence were initiated by a confidential report to the Colonial Office by the Governor of Nigeria in 1942. Administrative preparations were pushed on, even before the end of the War, and soon after its conclusion constitutions with a larger elective element were introduced in several colonies. In the Gold Coast and in Nigeria constitutions of a far more democratic character than any known previously in colonial Africa were introduced by the two governors, Sir Alan Burns and Sir Arthur Richards, respectively, in 1946 and 1947. They were not democratic enough for the Africans. A nationalist movement with an organization like that of the Indian National Congress, which just then was achieving independence in India, captured the imagination of the urban peoples in the commercialized towns of the Gold Coast. After riots had taken place in Accra, a commission was appointed under an African judge, Sir H. Coussey, to draft a stiil more advanced constitution. The nationalist leader, Dr Nkrumah, denounced it as insufficient, but was persuaded by a tactful Governor, Sir Charles Arden-Clarke, to accept it for what it was worth.[35] It is in the history of the Gold Coast from 1948 to the day of Ghanaian independence in 1957 that the dual nature of the political process by which British colonies attain to independence may most clearly be studied. On the one hand there was Dr Nkrumah, leading a "fight for liberation" and obliging the authorities to confine him in a prison from which he emerged a hero and a martyr; on the other hand there was the colonial administration, patiently preparing the steps by which he advanced towards the goal which both had in view. The Ghana Constitution of 1957 was designed as an exact adjustment of the British parliamentary system to the needs of an African state. It was modified by provisions for preserving the status of the tribal chiefs, although at a colonial conference in England in 1947 the principle of indirect rule had virtually been abandoned. Nevertheless, there were tribal associations in Ghana, notably the Ashanti Confederacy, which were thought likely to maintain their coherence even in a democracy. This belief proved illusory for Dr Nkrumah found it as easy to impose state authority on the Ashantis as Mr Nehru had found it to incorporate the ruling Indian princes into his regime. Ghana became independent in March 1957, and within three years the constitutional limitations on the power of the Ghanaian Government had been swept away.[36]

Far more complex problems emerged in the great state of Nigeria, four times as large and seven times as populous as Ghana. The Richards Constitution had for the first time brought the emirates of the Northern Region into the political field by creating a single legislative council with an elective element. A true political situation soon emerged in which regional differences had to be reconciled by negotiation, while in the more sophisticated south political parties to some extent overran regional boundaries. Constitutional progress almost inevitably took the form of a move towards federation with some danger, at one stage, that this great artificial state would fly to pieces. In 1953 and 1954 skilled negotiation by Mr Lyttelton, the Secretary of State for the Colonies, led to the deliberate planning of moves towards a federation which was to become independent in 1960. The Nigerian leaders, not unaware of errors made through precipitancy in Ghana, became increasingly willing to proceed with caution.

Since the Indian princes and Ashanti chiefs had failed to make any effective defence of their status, the British Government was misled into supposing that in Africa and Asia democracy meant an end to the mystique of monarchy. But an attempt to deprive the Malayan sultans of their prerogatives in 1946 had failed, and a high-handed interference with the Bamangwato chief in Bechuanaland produced troublesome reactions. In 1953 a liberal-minded governor of Uganda suspended and banished the Kabaka, the ruling member of a three-hundred-year-old dynasty which for three generations had been under the protection of the British crown. This was Coronation year in Britain, and no one should have been surprised when the Baganda people rallied around their traditional ruler instead of adhering to one of the political demagogues who abounded in their country as elsewhere in Africa. Though this purely native reaction demonstrated a healthy sociological tendency—that is, that indigenous traditions had not been destroyed by foreign influences—it was a reminder that the tensions created by the impact of Europe on Africa were not uniform. Expatriate notions were neither widespread nor deeply felt except among the detribalized Africans of the towns.

East Africa, on the whole, was far more primitive than West Africa, except where some enclave of white settlers had established their imported culture. Against this particoloured social system one African reaction took the form of a total rejection of the civilized life of the West, and erupted in mere barbarism, an orgiastic return to the primitive. This was the Mau Mau movement of Kenya, which was directed against the civilized, co-operating Africans rather than the European immigrants. It was put down by force which would not have been effective if the mass of more civilized Africans had not rallied to the side of progress and decency.

But federalism, which had solved so many colonial problems in the past, and which was making headway in Nigeria, could not be so easily adjusted to the multi-racial societies of southern and eastern Africa, where the differences in economic and social advancement between the various groups had more ultimate reality than the racial distinctions upon which emotional fervour was focused. In the Union of South Africa power had long since passed away from the imperial authorities, and the problems of *apartheid*, so widely denounced and so narrowly understood, seemed to poison the atmosphere and to breed ill will. In Central Africa a well-established white colony already enjoyed the civil rights that Ontario and Nova Scotia had enjoyed at the same stage of their history, and now demanded the same opportunity for self-government. How were the authentic rights of this settlement-colony to be reconciled with those of the surrounding Africans, twelve times as numerous but members of a community which had become viable only because of European techniques and European investments? Rightly or wrongly, the first steps towards forming a federation were taken between 1951 and 1953 with consequences that were irrevocable. Any later attempt to restrain the colonial government or to reverse the course of policy would entail discussion[37] in the Parliament of Westminster, where, most unfortunately, Central African policy had become a party issue.

Formidable and complex as were the problems of the Rhodesias they were surpassed in these respects by the problems of East Africa, a range of territories which, to the tidy-minded, seemed to demand some sort of federal plan. The Africans, particularly in Uganda, objected even to the creation, in 1948, of the East African High Commission, which was designed to provide them with some common public services, notably in transportation. The fear of domination by a white settler group lurked in every African mind in spite of the 1923 declaration of African 'paramountcy' which had been so often renewed and was reaffirmed at the conference in February 1960.

Ghana, which became independent in 1957, and the Federation of Nigeria, which became independent in 1961,

E

are all-African states, closely linked with Europe and dependent upon Atlantic trade. East Africa, with its ports on the Indian Ocean and its Asian immigrant population, belongs to another geographical region. East and West Africa have no direct communications, no trade relations, and no common language except English. The African 'presence,' if it really exists, is to be found only in the field of active political organization. Skin-colour, to which enlightened persons in the West have long since ceased to attach any importance, recognizing that it is not associated with any distinctive mental quality, is valued in Africa as the visible symbol of Africanism. Time was when the white man was master and when all white men's values prevailed. We are now in an equally irrational age. Black men band together to extol the virtues which are believed to be peculiar to dark-skinned people. Racialism has been made part of the platform of African political leaders, and we white men have no moral right to condemn them for exploiting, in their turn, this potent emotional appeal.

While British colonial Africa moved into this phase of political liveliness, the world supposed that the other parts of Africa were still unawakened. Rather to the astonishment of outside observers, all the tensions which had distracted Ghana and Nigeria appeared in not dissimilar forms in French West Africa in 1957 and even in Belgian Africa in 1958. The French Union, which had seemed so stable ten years earlier, broke up into its constituent parts as soon as the *Loi Cadre* of 1956 enabled the African territories to modify their own constitutions in accordance with resolutions voted by universal suffrage. The French Union, too, had its white settler problem in Algeria, and its combinations of provinces hesitating whether to federate or not. The difference between French and British colonial Africa lay in the closer attachment of the *évolués*, the educated French Africans, to the cultural life of Paris, and in the rigorous, not to say brusque, rationality with which De Gaulle made his decisions. They might stay as Frenchmen in the *communauté* or go into an independence which meant outer darkness—excommunication.

De Gaulle and his African friends were set upon preserving the French 'presence' in Africa; the British were content to let the traditional Commonwealth bonds hold the new independent countries in what had been British colonial Africa in a free association with Britain. Of late, however, a growing sense of an African 'presence' above and beyond the distinctions between those Africans who have no common language but French and those who have none but English is being fostered in every newly independent state.

# III

# The Last Phase

NOW that the process of change from Empire to Commonwealth is almost complete we are in a position to draw up a provisional balance sheet. The United Kingdom has lost the pride of place it once enjoyed on account of its overseas Dominions, which made it the most powerful state in the world. But, having relinquished its possessions, it has also escaped the jealous rage against imperial power which is the prevailing attitude to-day, and it has won some credit for bringing to birth a new group of nation-states which retain certain advantageous associations with one another although they are widely separated. It may be claimed that Britain is still much more than a small island in the North Atlantic. It will not serve to describe the British in the terms that have been used of the Spanish as "empire-builders gone out of business," since the British have not forfeited their assets nor repudiated their liabilities. The Commonwealth actually exists in a new mode which I have now to examine.

But first it will be helpful to beat the bounds of this parcelled-out estate, and assess what the liquidation of the British Empire means, locality by locality. Let us begin with some dead losses. Ireland and Burma, a European and an Asian state, insisted upon complete political severance when they reached the final stage of self-government, and were allowed to withdraw without rancour. The long, sad history of Anglo-Irish relations perhaps precluded any other solution of the political problem as it stood in 1949. A period of isolationism may yet appease the inherited Irish wrath, and, by way of internationalism rather than imperialism, the Irish may yet return to some form of political co-operation with the neighbour upon whose economy they are still dependent. Meanwhile, in citizenship, in tariff preferences, and in many professional associations, the Irish and the British enjoy reciprocal advantages of various kinds which scarcely differ from those shared by Commonwealth countries. We, at least, refuse to regard the Irish as foreigners.

It was of Burma that Lord Attlee was speaking when he said that we want no unwilling members in the Commonwealth.[1] Here there was no legacy of hate to poison the negotiations, no ancient grudge that would be satisfied only by a defiant gesture of separation. Timing is always the decisive factor in politics, and if the independence of Burma had been achieved after that of India, instead of before it, Burma might well have followed India's example by becoming a republic within the Commonwealth. Perhaps not! The Burmese secession, while we may regret it for the Commonwealth as a whole, and may even regard it as a minor misfortune for Burma, has its historic value in that it proved the reality of Commonwealth independence. If Burma could leave without ill-feeling on either side, then the liquidation of Empire was genuine; and if the other Asian countries decided to remain with us, then continuing Commonwealth co-operation was genuine.

It is on turning from farther Asia to nearer Asia that the heart of the Commonwealth apologist faints within him. If Britain was responsible for the formation of the two states of Iraq and Jordan it was also responsible for the Palestine mandate, and in what company are we to claim credit for both? What Egypt owes to seventy years of British protection and development is best not alluded to while Egyptian politicians are still so enflamed by the errors of our policy at Suez. Yet our history is studded with the shining names of true heroes—Gordon, Cromer, Kitchener, Lawrence, Allenby—whom future historians will replace upon their pedestals when the anti-colonial frenzy of the present generation has died away. They will be remembered as the creators of the states whose rulers now react so sharply against the traditions that their names recall. Why have the material infra-structure of trade and communications and the moral infra-structure of political ideas and cultural standards fallen to pieces in the Arab world while they survived the change from Empire to Commonwealth unscathed in many more distant countries? This question is too urgent and contemporary to be answered by an historian. The Commonwealth is in eclipse in the Near East in 1960, and it will be pleasanter and more profitable to look at countries where it is regarded more favourably.

Nigeria has moved to independent status after confronting new variants of the old problems that Canada solved a century ago, with a like prudence and moderation. We may hope that the West Indies will do as well. But the major crisis of our day is concerned with the multi-racial states in the eastern half of Africa, to which allusion was made in the last chapter.

If the formidable problems facing these states are solved, or if the warring interests there can be so far reconciled as to allow for the beneficent influence of time and patience, have we then reached the conclusion of our story? Is the British Empire liquidated? No, indeed! Many new problems remain to be faced, and it will be well if they can be treated as Commonwealth problems, not as administrative embarrassments for the Government of the United Kingdom.

Let us first look at the residue of very small colonies which seem unlikely to survive as viable, independent nation-states. The League of Nations was founded in 1920 with forty-two members, and it would have been thought complete, after Germany and Soviet Russia had been admitted, if the United States could have been induced to join. The United Nations started with a membership of fifty-one, which has now increased to eighty-three, with a prospect of about ten more states, mostly small and weak, likely to claim admission. The Balkanization of the world, which the statesmen at Versailles forty years ago so prudently deprecated, seems to have taken place. What is the smallest practicable size for a sovereign nation-state? Why not admit Monaco, Andorra, and San Marino to the roll? In what real sense is the vote of Iceland, with its population of 160,000, to be equated with the vote of the United States, where the population exceeds 160,000,000? Nor is size the only criterion of world status. How can any comparison be drawn between Soviet Russia, where the gigantic bureaucratic system is controlled and directed with superlative efficiency by the self-appointed leaders of a party which is identified with the state, and a new-born community like the French Cameroons, where the president's authority hardly extended beyond his capital city on

Independence Day? British colonial policy has now been concerned for so many years with combining smaller territories into larger, viable unions or federations, that little thought has been given to the dispersed territories and islands which do not easily arrange themselves in groups.

The independence of British Somaliland, hurriedly brought about in June 1960, was a departure from the old rule. No one could suppose that this backward territory, so poor in economic resources, so ill-provided with educated citizens, was a viable community, or that it was more ready to pass out of tutelage into sovereign statehood than several African colonies which were slowly moving along the well-trodden path. British Somaliland was encouraged to anticipate the others for reasons of external politics, because the neighbouring state of Somalia was moving on a pre-arranged time-table towards its independence. Two non-viable states, with an expressed intention to combine, were assumed to strengthen one another's claims. Britain's rather precipitate withdrawal is not the most glorious episode in the liquidation of the Empire.

The well-established colony of Sierra Leone, celebrated for its schools and its century-old college at Fourah Bay, has a better claim to become a nation-state than several small territories which have recently attained to membership of the United Nations. The promise of full self-government within the Commonwealth which has recently been given could hardly have been withheld. The population of Sierra Leone is about two millions, many of them, in the interior, still quite primitive. How much farther is this process of devolution to be taken? British Guiana, which has received a similar promise, has no more than half a million inhabitants and among them a racial issue.

British Guiana, Mauritius, and Fiji might not seem at a first glance to have much in common. But each of them by the immigration of Asians has created a multi-racial society with the inevitable rivalries and divisions. Each of these three countries has, actually or potentially, a prosperous economy, and in none of them is the social tension as dangerous as in tropical Africa. Yet, if trouble comes in these countries it is only the Imperial power that can be invoked to impose a settlement. The year 1960 has shown, in the Congo, what greater misfortunes may spring from a premature withdrawal of the colonial administration. What would be the most effective method of providing for these smaller emergent colonies if a systematic plan could be devised for the residue of the British Empire? It is easy to propose regional solutions. Instead of being hustled into independence it would be better for the peoples of these territories if they could be hustled into some sort of confederation with neighbouring Commonwealth countries: British Guiana into the West Indian Federation, Mauritius into the sphere of the East African High Commission, Fiji into association with Australia—that is, if they would accept the authority of these larger bodies, and if the larger bodies would accept the responsibility. However this general problem is approached, a stubborn residue of smaller colonies confronts us:

|  | *Approximate Population in 1960* |
|---|---|
| Hong Kong | 2,500,000 |
| Singapore | 1,500,000 |
| North Borneo, Brunei, and Sarawak | 1,000,000 |
| Aden and the protectorates | 800,000 |
| Mauritius | 550,000 |
| Fiji | 500,000 |

|  | *Approximate Population in 1960* |
|---|---|
| Malta | 320,000 |
| Western Pacific islands | 250,000 |
| Bahamas | 100,000 |
| British Honduras | 80,000 |
| Bermuda | 40,000 |
| Seychelles | 40,000 |
| Gibraltar | 25,000 |
| St Helena | 5,000 |
| Falkland Islands and dependencies | 2,000 |

In this list there is one true nation, though it has never been a nation-state. The Maltese are a homogeneous people unlike any other in the world; they have a language and a culture to which they are strongly attached, religious unity, and a memorable history reaching back into remote antiquity. Their numerous friends regret the incomprehensible dispute in which (at the time these words are written) Maltese affairs have become entangled. This is the test case of the very small nation. In no foreseeable circumstances could Malta be self-supporting or self-reliant; as throughout history, so in the future the island must be associated with some external power or combination of powers, and it is certainly our wish that it should continue to be associated with the Commonwealth.

North Borneo, Brunei, and Sarawak seem suited by their geographic position for forming a federal union (some efforts have already been made in this direction), but Brunei is rich with oil, while the other two are poor, and the Sultan of Brunei seems to be inclined to co-operate with his fellow sultans in the Malayan Federation rather than with his more primitive neighbours. Though Singapore would like to join the same group, the Malayans do not favour the prospect of incorporating an international sea-port with a majority of immigrant Chinese. Self-government and re-integration have progressed in the Malayan region since the expulsion of the Japanese. With time, and patience—rare commodities, but better understood in Asia than in Africa—a Greater Malaya may yet emerge.

Last on my list come the Falkland Islands and their dependencies. Since these lectures were delivered a treaty has been signed between all the powers having territorial claims or scientific interests in the Antarctic Continent.[2] They are to co-operate and to share information, through a continuing international scientific body, for thirty years, during which time all territorial claims will be suspended. The futile triangular scuffling over South Georgia between Britain, Chile, and the Argentine, three states which have no other cause of quarrel, will be stopped; and all three will be relieved of the fear of encroachment by the U.S.A. or the U.S.S.R. This is far from being, as yet, the international control of a colonial region; but it is at least an interim agreement by an international body on the solution of a colonial problem. The Powers are combining, for practical reasons, to share the frozen wastes of Antarctica instead of standing firm on questionable claims to territory. This might set a precedence for the international approach to territorial problems in the light of strictly practical considerations, without regard to formalities or national prestige.

No doubt sceptics will observe that no issues of vital importance to the signatories were involved; if the numerous expeditions to Antarctica during the International Geophysical Year had produced evidence of some strategic advantage to be gained by making lodgments in that region the international agreement would not have been so easily reached. This brings us to the strategic factor in Common-wealth affairs.

The defence policy of the United Kingdom, as set forth in the annual White Papers issued to justify the estimates of money voted by parliament to the armed services,[3] has three distinct elements. First it is concerned with the obligations laid upon the British under the series of international defensive treaties—that is to say, commitments to NATO, CENTO, SEATO, and to some allied and protected states. These are explicit obligations undertaken by the Government of the United Kingdom in accordance with international law and within the terms of the United Nations Charter. Some Commonwealth countries are bound by some of these defensive treaties and others are not. For example, Canada is a member of NATO but Australia is not; Australia is a member of SEATO but Canada is not; and it is worth noting at this point, that while the United Kingdom is a member of both NATO and SEATO, it is not a member of the ANZUS pact to which Australia and New Zealand adhere. India belongs to none of these organizations. It is thus plain that the system of treaties is quite distinct from the Commonwealth system, and that the two are not directly involved with one another. Having said so, we turn to the second element in the defence policy of the United Kingdom and find that there is also a vague but perceptible Commonwealth commitment. A body of troops known as the Commonwealth Strategic Reserve, including contingents from Australia and New Zealand, is stationed in the Malayan region, and is, to some extent, directed by a staff organization called ANZAM, about which few particulars have been given to the public.

If Australia were to become engaged in a war in the Eastern Hemisphere outside the zone that is covered by SEATO under the Treaty of Manila, is it not obvious that she could count on some military help from Britain? If India were subjected to attacks from China in another incident resembling the Korean incident of 1950, could she not also count on British help? In the first instance there is little doubt that Commonwealth unity would reveal itself; in the second instance this would not be so sure. But if the Government of the United Kingdom were to give support to India in accordance with a majority decision of the United Nations, we should see the reappearance of a phenomenon as in the Korean War, about which I shall have more to say presently. The association of the Commonwealth armed forces in military education, administration, and logistics would, without doubt, lead to an effective and close co-operation.

The limiting factor in the use of the so-called Commonwealth Strategic Reserve is the maintenance of staging-posts across the world, that is to say in the network of smaller strategic colonies. Their defence provides the third element of British policy, which will become clear if we examine the position of NATO in the Mediterranean, where it joins hands with CENTO.

The strength of NATO in the Mediterranean rests upon the American Sixth Fleet and upon the British bases that survive from the days of the British Empire. For seventy years or more the strategic control of the Old World, except that of Western Europe, rested ultimately upon British sea power, which, in turn, rested upon a chain of strategic posts—Gibraltar, Malta, Suez, Aden, Trinkomali, Singapore—covering the direct sea route to the Far East.

A painful alternative route around Africa by way of Free-town and Simonstown could be used as a last resort. In those days a world-wide system of dockyards, bases, and cable communications was of decisive strategic importance in war and a great commercial advantage in peace. This system of bases was the articulation of the British Empire, and its influence on world affairs was wholly beneficent, since it served, and could serve, no purpose but to promote peace and plenty.

Strategically, its first importance lay in the fact that it was the link between the two main striking forces of the old British Empire, the Navy based on its home ports and the Army based on India. India's adoption of a neutralist policy and its refusal to join SEATO has left a strategic vacuum in western Asia. Formerly Britain's interest in Suez lay in the commercial and strategic links it provided with India; the Canal was part of a world system of communications. To-day Britain is interested in the Canal as a supply route for the oil brought from the Persian Gulf for the use of Western Europe.

> Outside the area covered by the North Atlantic Alliance, Britain has military responsibilities in other parts of the world, in particular of the Middle East and South-east Asia. Apart from its own importance, the Middle East guards the right flank of NATO and is the gateway to the African continent. In the Arabian peninsula, Britain must at all times be ready to defend Aden Colony and Protectorates and the territories on the Persian Gulf for whose defence she is responsible. For this task, land, sea, and air forces have to be maintained in that area and in East Africa. In addition, Britain has undertaken in the Baghdad Pact to co-operate with the other signatory states.
>
> In South-east Asia, apart from defending her colonies and

protectorates, Britain has agreed to assist in the external defence of Malaya after she attains independence. Britain also has an international commitment, as a member of the SEATO and ANZAM defence systems, to help preserve stability and resist the extension of communist power in that area. It is proposed to maintain in this theatre [*sic*] a mixed British-Gurkha force and certain air force elements, together with a substantial garrison in Hong Kong and a small naval force based on Singapore.[4]

I cannot avoid the conclusion that the framers of Britain's defence policy have failed to take the same step forward from Empire to Commonwealth that has been taken in other political departments. How can there be a Commonwealth Strategic Reserve when there is no Commonwealth strategic policy and, indeed, when there is a very strong objection on the part of two or three members against having such a policy? Many people may think that there ought to be a Commonwealth strategy and a body of troops to implement it, but they must first convince the neutralists. Meanwhile the strategic infra-structure crumbles. Cyprus is a poor substitute for Suez, and the Maldive staging-post is no substitute at all for the island of Ceylon. The weakness of these new strategic posts is that they are unrelated to any working machinery that the Commonwealth possesses. Why is the British taxpayer to be mulcted for their upkeep when Britain no longer rules a world-wide empire? What world-wide interest has the United Kingdom other than a Commonwealth interest?

A single defence policy for the Commonwealth has been impracticable since the Imperial Conference of 1937 when it was agreed that it was " the sole responsibility of the several parliaments of the British Commonwealth to decide the nature and scope of their own defence arrangements."[5]

This decision was put to the test by Mr Mackenzie King, who had previously announced that "Canada would take no action in a European war without a reference of all the existing circumstances to his parliament." Until the very outbreak of war in 1939 he insisted upon Canada's right to be neutral if she chose and abstained from open and public co-operation with the United Kingdom, though it is fair to say that the military planners committed the Canadian forces to some secret preliminary measures which would have made neutrality difficult.[6] However, the Canadian Government did not formally declare war on Germany until Parliament had debated the situation, a week after the declaration by the United Kingdom.

By the end of the Second World War the United States dominated both parts of the Grand Alliance. The United States, the United Kingdom, and Canada sustained the western front in Europe; the United States, the United Kingdom, Australia, New Zealand, and India sustained the Japanese war. Canada and Australia respectively complied with a world strategy prescribed by the Combined Chiefs of Staff at Washington. The very notion of an Imperial defence policy was lost and has not been recovered.

When next the Commonwealth countries combined to make a joint military effort it was under international not Imperial auspices; the Korean War is an important landmark in Commonwealth affairs. The invasion of Korea was begun on June 25, 1950, and on the same day was denounced as aggression by the Security Council. On the 27th President Truman authorized General MacArthur to act, and on the 28th Mr Attlee placed the available elements of the Royal Navy at MacArthur's disposal. Ships and aircraft from Canada, Australia, and New Zealand were in action during July, and a British infantry brigade landed in Korea in August. The different Commonwealth countries made their offers of help to the United Nations force separately, and, though there had been previous consultations, their decisions were taken so swiftly that there cannot have been time for much discussion among them between the dates of the invasion and of the reaction against it. On June 29 Mr Attlee spoke in the House of Commons on the "striking unity displayed by Commonwealth Members."[7] All of them, except Ceylon (which was not a member of the United Nations), had agreed to the resolution condemning North Korea as the aggressor; and all of them, except Pakistan and Ceylon, made some contribution to the war effort. Even India, with its strongly pacifist and neutralist tendencies, sent a field ambulance unit which, once in the field, joined without demur in the organization set up by the other Commonwealth countries. Between June 1950 and May 1951[8] military units from the United Kingdom, Canada, Australia, New Zealand, and India were gradually grouped together in a single formation which, in July 1951, became the Commonwealth Division under a British commander with an integrated staff (including South African officers). Administratively, it grew out of the Commonwealth Occupation Force in Japan, in which there was already a high degree of co-operation among units from various countries in the Commonwealth. When this Force grew larger, its main base was established in Japan, and there an Australian general was appointed commander-in-chief of the Commonwealth forces in Korea. The Commonwealth Division was frequently in action and lost 1200 men before the armistice of July 1953. In 1955 it was reduced to a brigade group, and in 1956 the base in Japan was

F

closed. The creation and operation of the Commonwealth Division has been the most perfect example so far of Commonwealth co-operation in war.

For the independent Commonwealth countries, strategic policy is likely to be regional in character and to be implemented through the procedures of the United Nations. On the other hand, co-operation for any specific purpose will be most effective, as it was in Korea, if use can be made of the Commonwealth infra-structure, the network of communication lines and bases that runs through the whole geographical field of the former British Empire and relies particularly upon such centres as Singapore. The smaller colonies acquired in the nineteenth century were annexed usually to serve as communication links, as staging-posts, as fuelling bases, as dockyards, as munitions depots, as relay posts for the mails, and above all as terminals for the trans-oceanic cables which bound the whole trading empire together. It would not be merely fanciful to describe the British Empire as a web of submarine telegraph cables. Modern international trade began when world prices could be quoted over the telegraph, when shippers could notify owners that a cargo was on the way, and when mercantile agents abroad could be briefed quickly by their employers; and the world's cable system is built upon terminals in Commonwealth countries, administered by the Commonwealth Telecommunications Board. Some years ago it seemed that beam wireless and air transportation might change the existing patterns of communication and trade; on the contrary, they have strengthened them; trade has been so effectively channelled into certain lines that air and radio connexions can do nothing but follow the same lines.

Before we leave the question of Commonwealth strategy

we should glance again at the future of the smaller colonies, the nodal points in the network of communications. Taken singly, they are insignificant; maintained in their places as vital members of a world-wide system, they will continue to flourish. Take Singapore, for instance. The people of Singapore enjoy the highest standard of living in Asia because it is a link in an international trading system. To the United Kingdom, now that the British no longer possess a world-wide empire, Singapore has no material importance except as a centre for long-distance overseas trade. It is not to retain possession of Singapore Island that the British pay taxes, but to maintain the complex of trading facilities at Singapore by which they, the people of Singapore, and indeed all the people of South-east Asia, may hope to prosper. For the sake of the sterling trade its defence is strategically important to the whole Commonwealth.

Nothing but peace and plenty could be the interest of the nation of shopkeepers who have built trading connexions all over the world, not only to their own great advantage, but to the great advantage of their customers. The trade which passes along the old lines of communication steadily increases in volume, and that is the only criterion upon which any stable judgment of the efficiency of the old system can be formed. From time to time voices are heard lamenting that the sterling Commonwealth trade is declining in proportion to total world trade, and that therefore Britain is in some sense losing ground. Precisely the contrary is true. As Adam Smith pointed out nearly two hundred years ago, the endeavour to monopolize trade by making Imperial trade a closed circuit was not only bad policy, it was bad business and "unworthy of a nation of shopkeepers." It paid Britain best to traffic with the rich, and accordingly to help its clients to grow rich. The wisest statesmen of King George III's day[9] realized that Britain might do better business with a free America than it had ever done with subject colonies, as indeed it has done, so that the United States is still its best customer. Trade made Britain rich and laid the foundation of American prosperity. We have seen the same process at work in Australia and Canada, and we hope to see it continue in Ghana and Malaya. So much for the myth of exploitation.

The secret of this continuing and growing trade is that it too is founded upon a firm and time-tested infra-structure. Complaints are sometimes heard, on both sides of the Atlantic, that Canada's freedom has been short-lived; it has passed out of British Imperial control only to fall under the economic control of the United States, with whom it conducts three-quarters of its external trade and from whom it draws three-quarters of its imported capital. It is salutary to notice that the east-west commerce in wheat along the old trade-route from Winnipeg to Liverpool remains remarkably steady. An average of 41,000,000 hundredweights passed that way in the three years 1936, 1937, and 1938, and an average of 67,000,000 in 1956, 1957, and 1958. No one can describe this as a decline, though it represents a much smaller fraction of Canada's total trade than it did before the war. The stability of the old trade is the foundation upon which the new trade grows.

There would be no such stability if it were not for the factors that are classified by the economists as invisible, a strangely undescriptive term because the docks, warehouses, railway sidings, airports, cable stations, banking houses, insurance offices, ships seaborne, and aircraft airborne are the most plainly visible evidences of the world-wide sterling system, centred upon London and operated for the advantage of all its users. It is unique in the world, and without it not only might Britain be as poor as Spain, but Rhodesia, Nigeria, and the other emergent countries would lose the means of advancement.

From the factors in trade technically described as the invisibles we may well turn to the immaterial bonds of the Commonwealth, "lighter than air but stronger than steel," about which so many speeches have been delivered on public platforms. Some recent critics have even suggested that the Commonwealth no longer exists in any other mode, that it has no real value except as a repository of fading traditional loyalties. A witty Frenchman has written:

> I do not know how long it will take the British to notice that the Commonwealth is no longer anything more than an Old Boys' Association which meets every year. . . . Everybody asks what everybody else has been doing for the last twelve months; everybody says, "What are you going to to do to-morrow, old chap!" Then each one goes home and does what he likes. [10]

While it would be misleading to ignore the reality or the strength of sentiment in the Commonwealth connexion it is wholly wrong to suggest that the Commonwealth is not based upon any more solid foundation. To think of the Commonwealth as a political organization of nations which meet and confer only at the occasional conferences of their prime ministers is to ignore the rich tissue of social, economic, and administrative threads which connect these affiliated countries and are woven intimately into their national lives. These nations co-operate because history has provided them with common objectives and common interests. If the political principles on which their association is built were to be enunciated they might be stated in terms such as these:

1. The Commonwealth is in continuous session. As well as taking part in the occasional high-level conferences which attract public notice, the members maintain daily contact with one another through the Commonwealth Relations Office. The duties of this office include the exchange of confidential information and the arrangement of direct consultations between members upon any subject of interest, through all departments, and at all appropriate levels.

2. The Commonwealth rejects the principle of majority rule in its deliberations. It does not act as a sovereign body, taking all political questions into its cognizance with the intention of forming a plan of action to which all must adhere or resign. It directs its attention to finding the highest measure of agreement among members on specific issues. No effort is made to coerce minorities.

3. In major political crises, after the usual consultation has taken place, decisions are made separately by Commonwealth countries in their capacity as sovereign states, not collectively by all as a Commonwealth group.

4. When a number of Commonwealth countries have agreed upon joint action (whether in accordance with a United Nations decision or independently) administrative co-operation follows and an integrated staff is established.

The view commonly taken of the history of the British Empire during the last fifty or sixty years is that it is a tale of disintegration, of the splitting up of an overgrown conglomeration into its component parts. But nation-

states are not fixed, immutable creations like the biological
species of the older scientists. The British Empire included
some ancient realms which have resumed their former
independence; it includes more countries which have been
engendered and brought to birth by British administrators,
usually through the patient combination of groups of small,
weak societies into larger and stronger units. Two processes have been at work: the building up of new states
from below and the decentralization of power from above.
Decentralization is not the same thing as disintegration.
The growth of the Commonwealth has been an administrative process at least as much as it has been a political
process: the real problem in the transfer of power has been
to decide when, and to whom, power should be transferred.
Self-determination by democratic process often came at
the end of the story, after the nation had been created. In
politics, and in other fields, the process of decentralization
has been continuous, often far more advanced in economics
than in politics. When the transfer of power was completed,
energies which political leaders had previously devoted to
the cause of hastening independence were released for
direction towards more productive ends. It is our study
(and our pride) that they have sometimes been used to
develop new forms of Commonwealth co-operation which
are more effective than those sponsored under the old
Imperial control. Political goodwill enables administrative
co-operation to continue. If the Commonwealth has a
message for the world it is this: concentrate upon administrative co-operation with all friendly peoples for immediate
practical ends. This is almost the converse of the principle
of democratic centralization in the communist countries,
where deviation from a decision once taken is a crime.

# APPENDIX

## Constitutional Theory in 1791

The parliamentary debates on the Constitutional Act of 1791 deserve a moment's attention.[1] On February 25 Pitt presented to the House of Commons a message from the King acquainting them of his recommendation that the Province of Quebec should be divided in two, and that in each part provision should be made for supporting and maintaining the Protestant clergy with an endowment of land. This was the origin of the clergy reserves which were to be so large an issue in Canadian politics during the next two generations. Nothing was said in the King's message about the form of government to be adopted in the two Canadian provinces.

The Quebec Government Bill was accordingly prepared and was debated in the House of Commons on April 8 at the report stage. An amendment was moved "that the Bill do lie on the table," by a member speaking for the merchants of Quebec, who feared that they would lose by the Bill. Fox seconded the motion and spoke at length on the faults that he detected in the new constitution. The provincial assemblies would be too small to give adequate representation; the qualification for the franchise was too high; the clergy reserves ought to provide for the Scottish church as well as for the English; the intention to create an hereditary aristocracy in Canada would "stink in the nostrils of the natives." He suggested that in framing a constitution for Canada British legislators might learn something from the constitution of the United States or even from the new reformed monarchy in France. In replying, Pitt showed himself willing to make concessions, but he thought "the English constitution was best for us, better than any of those republican principles." Experience would teach the Canadians "that the English laws were the best." The Bill was then ordered to be recommitted.

It came up for debate again on April 21 and occupied the attention of the House for many hours. But the proceedings opened with a comment that is only too frequent in the history of colonial Bills. Sheridan protested that so important a measure should not be taken in so thin a house "immediately before the holidays." The debate should be postponed and more time given to members for consideration. Pitt, however, refused to give way in view of the fact that the Bill had been examined in committee and had met with "so little opposition." The lead was taken by Fox, who again referred to the situation in France: "Some attention should be paid," he said, "to the general principles of all governments." This remark was fatal to the progress of the debate. During the previous days a personal quarrel over the news from France had taken place between Fox and Burke, two lifelong associates and friends. Fox, who had once thought the fall of the Bastille the "greatest and best thing that had ever happened," rejoiced that the French now had a constitution founded upon the rights of man, and said so in the debates on the Canadian Bill. Burke had just published his *Reflections on the Revolution in France*, in which, at that early date, before the fall of the monarchy, before the September Massacres and long before the Reign of Terror, he had foreseen and denounced the chaos and bloodshed through which France must pass. The mere mention of French principles as a guide to lawgivers for Canada detonated him into ponderous eloquence on the woes of the French King and the French clergy, and into bitter personal attacks on Fox, who rose to protest, time after time, that he was no republican. No one could long recall Burke to the business before the House.

Several points of order were moved, with no other effect than to give Burke a new opportunity to take the floor. The amiable Fox was at last provoked into a counter-attack: it was his friend Burke, he said, who had taught him in the old days of the American War that one cannot "draw up an indictment against a whole nation." To this Burke replied with mounting violence, and appealed to the House to "flee from the French constitution" when legislating for Canada. At last, "with tears trickling down his cheeks," Fox begged his adversary not to sever their old friendship, but in vain. The episode ended comically. Fox left the House "to seek some trifling refreshment," whereupon the solid phalanx of his supporters, twenty or thirty in number, marched out, supposing this to be a political manœuvre, and came back no more that day. Burke accepted this as the sign of his severance from the Whig party, and renewed his denunciations. The Whig party was indeed split, with the consequence that the Tories held office, with one slight intermission, for forty years.

The debate was resumed with similar irrelevance on May 6 and 11. At each stage Pitt attempted to intervene with moderation and to insist that a mixed constitution for Canada, with an aristocratic element, would be the best safeguard against republican excesses. He quite failed to persuade the House to read the Bill clause by clause. Finally, they divided on two clauses: the provision for a hereditary upper chamber was carried by 88 votes to 39, that for restricting the numbers of the lower chamber by 91 to 40.

The most thoughtful comment was made by Henry Dundas, the Home Secretary, who said that "they could not pretend to give Canada the same constitution that they themselves lived under; all they could do was to lay the foundation for the same constitution, when increased population and time should have made the Canadians ripe to receive it."

The Bill was skilfully piloted through the House of Lords by Grenville, the Foreign Secretary (it is sometimes called Lord Grenville's Bill), on May 30. It was he who summed up the policy of the Government:

> It was undoubtedly a mistake to suppose that any government was free only as it approached to democratic principles. Absolute monarchy, absolute aristocracy, absolute democracy had been tried, and

each was found wanting. Our own constitution which was compounded of these three, was the envy of every surrounding nation. They were now about to communicate the blessings of the English constitution to the subjects of Canada, because they were fully convinced that it was the best in the world.

# Notes and References

## CHAPTER I

1. The famous phrase was used twice, at the Lord Mayor's Banquets in November 1942 and again in November 1943 (*The Times*, Nov. 11, 1942, and Nov. 10, 1943). On the first occasion it provoked a hostile comment from Mr Wendell Wilkie (*The Times*, Dec. 7, 1942). The second occasion seems more relevant to the Honkong issue.

2. See *Memoirs of Cordell Hull* (New York, 1948), vol. ii, p. 1596.

3. See C. E. Carrington in *International Affairs*, vol. xxxii, No. 4 (October 1956), p. 446.

4. British North America (No. 2) Act, 1949 (12, 13, and 14 Geo. VI, ch. 81).

5. Government of India Act, 1935 (26 Geo. V, ch. 2).

6. The Federation of Malaya Order in Council, 5.1.1957, No. 1534 made by virtue of The Federation of Malaya Independence Act, 1957 (5 and 6 Eliz. II, ch. 60).

7. James Bryce, *The American Commonwealth* (London, 1888).

8. Commonwealth of Australia Constitution Act, 1900 (63 and 64 Vict., ch. 12).

9. See the Objectives and Resolutions adopted by the Indian and Pakistani constituent assemblies in 1946 and 1949. N. Mansergh, *Documents and Speeches on British Commonwealth Affairs, 1931-1952* (Oxford, 1953), vol. ii, pp. 652 and 879.

10. J. Degras, *Soviet Documents* (Oxford, 1951), vol. i, pp. 9-11.

11. R. S. Baker, *Woodrow Wilson and World Settlement*

(London, 1923), p. 15. See also H. W. V. Temperley, *The History of the Peace Conference of Paris* (London, 1921), vol. iv, p. 429.

12. G. Murray in *Journal of the Royal Institute of International Affairs*, vol. i (December 1921), p. 13.

13. "Autonomous communities within the British Empire, equal in status, in no way subordinate one to another in any aspect of their domestic or external affairs . . . " *Report of the Imperial Conference*, 1926.

14. 31 Geo. III, ch. 31. Generally known as the Constitutional Act, properly the Quebec Government Act, 1791.

15. See Appendix, p. 88.

16. Lawrence was not consistent on this project. See *The Letters of T. E. Lawrence*, ed. D. Garnett (London, 1938), pp. 308 and 578.

## CHAPTER II

1. The incident is described in W. G. Blaikie, *Personal Life of David Livingstone* (London, 1880).

2. *The Times*, May 26, 1863.

3. *Parliamentary Papers, 1865*, vol. 412. See *Cambridge History of the British Empire* (Cambridge, 1940), vol. ii, p. 673.

4. See A. K. Cairncross, *Home and Foreign Investment* (Cambridge 1953). S. H. Frankel, *Capital Investment in Africa* (Oxford, 1938). W. H. B. Court in *Survey of British Commonwealth Affairs, 1918–1939* (London, 1940), Pt. I, vol. ii. J. A. Hobson invented the myth on an inadequate statistical basis in *Imperialism* (London, 1902); Lenin inflated it in various polemical works; Mr Strachey, in *The End of Empire* (London, 1959) merely repeats the Hobson-Lenin myth without using the statistics now available.

5. For the tortuous negotiations leading to these simple conclusions, see F. H. Hinsley, in *Cambridge History of the British Empire* (Cambridge, 1959), vol. iii, Chapters IV, VIII, and XIII; documentation in Sir E. Hertslet, the *Map of Africa by Treaty* (London, 1909) vol. ii.

6. The Convention of St Germain-en-Laye, September 10, 1919. *State Papers, 1919*, vol. cxii (London, 1922), p. 901. By the Treaty Establishing the European Economic community (Treaty of Rome) 1957, Article 131, the signatories agreed to bring into association with the Community the "Non-European countries and territories which have special relations with Belgium, France, Italy and the Netherlands." On this issue, see C. E. Carrington in *International Affairs*, vol. xxxvi. No. 4 (October 1960).

7. G. Bernard Shaw, *Fabianism and the Empire* (London, 1900).

8. Canada less ardently than the others, but a significant fact is that Queensland and New Zealand, the most advanced social democracies in the world, were the first to send contingents to South Africa.

9. J. S. Mill, *On Liberty* (London, 1859).

10. For the Montagu-Chelmsford Report see The *Cambridge History of the British Empire* (Cambridge, 1932), vol. v, pp. 589-594. For the Government of India Act, 1935 (26 Geo. V, ch. 2) see Mansergh, *Documents* (*op. cit.*), vol. i, pp. 254-292.

11. The present writer was shouted down at a Conservative conference in 1936 when he defended the policy of the Government of India Bill.

12. C. Headlam, *The Milner Papers: South Africa* (London, 1931-32), vol. ii, p. 542. Smuts to Milner, April 2, 1905.

13. J. P. R. Wallis, *One Man's Hand: the Story of Sir Charles Coghlan, First Premier of Southern Rhodesia* (London, 1950), pp. 183-194.

14. Sir William Blackstone, *Commentaries on the Laws of England* (1765), 4th ed. (London, 1876), vol. i, pp. 81-82.

15. *The Times* (London). Law Reports and leading article, July 30, 1918.

16. J. P. R. Wallis, *op. cit.*, pp. 200-215.

17. The leading case is Campbell *v.* Hall (1774). See *Parliamentary History* vol. xxix, pp. 655-658.

18. The evidence was analysed in the Morris Carter Report (*Kenya Land Commission* (London, 1934)) Cmd. 4556 and was

criticized in the Dow Report (*Royal Commission on East Africa*, 1953-55, Cmd. 9475).

19. Cmd. 1922.

20. *Hansard*, H. of L., vol. liv, July 26, 1923.

21. Figures based upon Lord Hailey, *An African Survey* (revised 1956). (Oxford, 1957), Chapter 11.

22. The best account is in S. E. Crowe, *The Berlin West African Conference* (London, 1942).

23. The Foreign Jurisdiction Acts (6 and 7 Vict. ch. 94, amended by 53 and 54 Vict. ch. 37, and consolidated by 3 and 4 Geo. V., ch. 16).

24. For the 'zoological gardens policy' or 'museum policy,' see *Problems of the Pacific*, Proceedings of the 4th Conference of the I.P.R. (Chicago, 1932), Chapter 12; also C. S. Belshaw, *Island Administration in the South-west Pacific* (London, 1950), pp. 73-75.

25. See Lord Hailey, *op. cit.*, p. 732.

26. For the Colonial Development and Welfare Debates see Hansard, H. of C., May 21, 1940, cols. 41-126. For recent statistics see the annual Command Papers. The latest is 1959, Cmd. 672.

27. *Report of the Commission on Higher Education in the Colonies*, 1945, The Asquith Report, Cmd. 6647.

28. Lord Hailey, *op. cit.*, p. 1226.

29. *Ibid.*, p. 1646.

30. Sir Charles Jeffries, *The Colonial Office* (London, 1955), p. xxiv.

31. Lord Cranborne (now Lord Salisbury) quoted in *The Colonial Empire*, 1947. Cmd. 7167.

32. *Charter of the United Nations* (1945). Art. 73.

33. *Hansard*, H. of C., Nov. 14, 1951.

34. The objectives of the Groundnuts Scheme were discussed in the House of Commons on November 6, 1947. *Hansard*, H. of C., vol. 443.

35. Accounts of the 'liberation' of Ghana, which do not belie one another in matters of fact, have been published by Dr K. Nkrumah. *Ghana Autobiography* (Edinburgh, 1957);

and by Sir Charles Arden-Clarke, last Governor of the Gold Coast, in *International Affairs* vol. xxxiv (January 1958).

36. The correct procedure for amending the constitution was followed as soon as Dr Nkrumah's government was assured of a sufficient majority. The entrenched clauses were removed by the Constitution (Repeal of Restrictions) Act, December, 1958. The revised constitution for a Republic of Ghana, which was submitted to a referendum in April 1960, though revolutionary in several respects, preserves the whole body of the common law.

37. See above. Note II, 17.

## CHAPTER III

1. Lord Attlee on Burmese independence. *Hansard*, H. of C., Dec. 20, 1946, col. 2342.

2. The final act of the conference on Antarctica was signed by all the interested powers on Dec. 5, 1959, Cmd. 913. At the date of writing these words (Feb. 1960) it had not been ratified by any power.

3. Notably Cmd. 124 (1957), and Cmd. 952 (1960).

4. Cmd. 124.

5. *Imperial Conference of 1937. Summary of Proceedings.* Cmd. 5482.

6. C. P. Stacey, *Official History of the Canadian Army* (Ottawa, 1955), vol. i, Chapter I.

7. *Hansard*, H. of C. vol. 416, cols. 2660-2661.

8. *Hansard*, H. of C. vol. 516, col. 973.

9. V. Harlow, *Founding of the Second British Empire* (London, 1952), vol. i, Chapter VI.

10. P. Delouvrier, in *European Integration*, ed. C. Grove Haines (Baltimore, 1957), p. 119.

## APPENDIX

1. All references in the Appendix are to the *Parliamentary History of England* (London, 1816), vol. xxviii, p. 1271; vol. xxix, pp. 104-399, 359-599, 656.